THE
BLUE COLLAR KING'S
BLUEPRINT
FOR SUCCESS

How to Create an
Abundantly Fulfilled Lifestyle and
Turn Your Service Business
Into an 8-Figure Cash Flow Machine

By MATT MURRAY

THE BLUE COLLAR KING'S BLUEPRINT FOR SUCCESS

BCK Results, LLC/October 2023

All rights reserved

Copyright © 2023 by Matt Murray

Cover Design by Aleesha Kanwal

Permission requests should be addressed in writing to:

Matt Murray at Matt@BlueCollarKing.com.

ISBN: 979-8-9894101-0-1

DEDICATION

I dedicate this book to my mom, Johane Murray.

I love you with all my heart!

Thank you for being the example of unconditional love, no matter how tough things can get in a family. You were always there for me, Scott and Stacey when we needed you most.

Thank you for being the example of unrelenting grit and never giving up on your dreams, never letting life's challenges defeat you, whether it be relationships, entrepreneurship, near-death motorhome accidents, cancer and the list could go on and on.

I am a byproduct of you, this book is a byproduct of you and all the people that I will touch in my lifetime will be better because you showed me how to be a stronger, better person, and to never give up, no matter how tough, how hard and how painfully miserable things can get.

TABLE OF CONTENTS

FOREWORD

Matt thought we were going to just sit and talk. LOL.

Within the first hour of Matt coming to Salt Lake City to work with me on his business he was turning green and puking in the parking lot. No joke, true story.

We hit the gym first thing in the morning for our first 1-on-1 coaching day and it started off with a BANG. We then went to my office where we quickly learned that Matt was falling apart all over the place. Business. Emotionally. At Home.

So we dug in. We dug in deep. We ripped all the Band-Aids© off and got to work. I thought Matt would leave my headquarters and either say "fuck that guy" and never come back, or it would change his life forever.

He chose the latter.

Matt went to work BIG. He stepped up. Week after week. Month after month. HE STAYED THE COURSE AND BUSTED HIS ASS TO CREATE THE LIFE HE WANTED.

He put the vices to bed, got powerful with his word, he owned his shit and he started the journey that I'm proud to say I have witnessed from the beginning, and ultimately has led to this book. I've been fortunate to have a front row seat to what is possible when a man gets hungry and focused, and Matt did just that.

I've seen the personal growth.

I've seen the business growth.

I've seen the marriage growth.

I've seen Matt grab ahold of the vision he had for the life he wanted and ruthlessly build it.

And that is why you should listen to him. He's DONE IT. He's damn near burned his whole world to the ground, and become the man to OWN HIS SHIT and fiercely and passionately build a bad ass life with his wife by his side. He ain't all talk. HE HAS BEEN IN THE TRENCHES, BLOODIED HIS KNUCKLES AND DUG HIS WAY OUT TO BUILD A GREAT LIFE.

He's human like the rest of us, and he sure ain't done building, but when Matt is speaking you should shut up and listen, and make sure you don't skim this book. READ IT. Soak it in. Learn from it.

And do the damn work just like Matt did.

~ Sean Whalen, Founder and CEO of Lions Not Sheep,
Best-Selling Author of "How to Make Sh*t Happen"

PREFACE

Are you hungry for something more than what you've currently got? I'm not just talking about profits and revenue. I'm talking about a life of true impact, a life where your business, your team and you yourself are functioning at peak potential. Is that what you *really* want? Whether you own a business or are a leader within one, I'd like to help you get the "something more" that seems just out of reach.

Why you need this book

Traditional business books often sugarcoat the challenges and don't get to the root of the real problems that are standing in the way of your success. This book does, and I sure don't sugarcoat things. Instead, I go way beyond quick fixes and vanity metrics to do a deep dive into what it takes to create sustainable growth on all levels – financially, emotionally and holistically.

Like I said, what do you really want? You probably picked up this book because every time you look at your business you realize that things aren't going as smoothly or growing as quickly as you'd like. You *know* that you can have more, that you want and deserve more and that there's a way to do it – you're just not sure what that way is.

That said, let's face it: The real "more" that we all strive for isn't just about more sales, more money in the bank and more of the financial security that money can bring. It's also about more fulfillment, more impact, more freedom and more fun.

My own wake-up call

I had been running my commercial HVAC/R business for over 15 years when I got to a place of fear and found myself making decisions based on trial and error. I kept trying stuff because I didn't have any confidence in what the next step should be. So it was a matter of, "Let me try this. Shoot, that didn't work. Okay, I'll try this other thing. Dang! I just lost a bunch of money on that one." And that pattern kept repeating.

Nothing seemed to work. It was like I had hit a ceiling of the limit of my abilities at the time. I tried all these different things, but I still couldn't expand or grow the business.

Then I took some time to do some reflection and analysis. And I realized that with all these different things I had tried – all the systems, tactics, books, marketing, sales, new people, new whatever – there was a common denominator: Me. "Fuck," I thought. "I'm the common denominator. The problem is me. *I'm* the leader of my life, business, family, health, etc. Everything is a byproduct of *my* capabilities as a human." And clearly my capabilities needed to expand.

It was one heck of a wake-up call.

So yeah, I get it. Taking that hard look at yourself isn't pleasant. Realizing that the problem is you can be brutal, but it's also the first step on a journey of personal and professional development that literally changes everything. Trust me, the initial discomfort is worth the reward on the other side.

What's holding *you* back?

Perhaps you've hit a ceiling, too. After all, like everyone else on this planet, you have blind spots and limitations. There are things you think you need and things you don't even know you need.

For example, you probably think that you need to grow your business and get more sales. But that's just like the top layer of the onion. Peel that layer back and what do you find? A need for trust, safety and a great environment where you, your team and your business can flourish.

Peel that layer back and now you have to ask: How do you create this great, flourishing environment? The answer is that you need a system, a blueprint for success that's tried and true.

So, what's holding you back? Chances are there are three things:

1. You're not doing anything to identify and overcome your blind spots and limitations.

2. You're staying hyper-focused on that "top layer of the onion," without realizing that there's a whole lot holding that layer up that also requires attention.

3. You don't have a structured system for approaching every aspect of your business and life.

Are you willing to change?

Here's the million-dollar question: Are you ready to do something about it? I don't just mean are you willing to read a book. I mean, are you willing to commit to a shift in perspective? Are you willing to leave behind methods and beliefs that aren't serving you and your business well? Or do you want to just keep doing things the way you've been doing them, with the information, training and systems (or lack thereof) that you currently have available, and keep getting the same results that you've been getting?

Think about it. Are you *really* willing to change how you approach your business and your life? Can you see the value in adopting a more structured, systematized approach to things? Have you even thought about why systems are so important?

Whether you realize it or not, systems govern everything. Your personal life, business, leadership style and more all require a systematized approach if you want to achieve meaningful improvement and sustainable/repeatable success. And here's the thing: The most successful people operate systematically. They see the world in terms of actionable, measurable outcomes. What this book provides is a holistic blueprint for such a systematic approach.

Is this book for you?

If you're content to continue on the current path, without growth or meaningful change, then this book is not for you. No hard feelings.

But if you consider yourself a blue collar maverick – someone who knows the value of hard work and is committed to making an impact – then you're precisely the person this book is for. If you're a blue collar business leader with a relentless desire to improve and impact, then I'm excited to help you make this happen.

Listen, the clock is ticking. Every day is an opportunity to redefine what you're capable of. You can choose to keep things status quo, or you can keep reading and opt for a change that could reshape your world. Which will it be?

MY STORY

I grew up in a blue-collar family, my parents grew up in blue-collar families, and their parents did, too. In fact, my parents met through their blue-collar jobs at a local grocery store where Mom was a cashier and Dad cut meat all day. No one in my family went to college, but they all worked very, very hard.

Growing up blue collar

Like all the other blue-collar families in my Southern California neighborhood, my family lived humbly. When I was a kid, Mom went to work, came home, made dinner and took care of my younger brother and me. She was a great, loving role model – always taking us places and having fun with us.

On top of his long hours as a meat cutter, Dad also found things to do in his spare time to make extra money. This is how he was able to buy fun things for our family, such as a used motorcycle or a boat with a blown-out motor that he could fix, so that we could have a boat. I remember being a little kid, standing in the garage with my Dad handing him tools out of his toolbox. We were always in the garage working on stuff, which I loved because I loved fixing things! I sure miss those days.

My parents taught me the value of hard work

By the time I was in junior high, Mom had had it with working in the grocery store. Of course, money-wise, not working was not an option. So my parents took a leap of faith, took out some loans and scraped together the money to buy the ice cream parlor / sandwich shop that was across the street from where we lived.

Because of this, at a very young age I got to see what it looks like for someone to be an entrepreneur. I think that it was by watching my parents at that ice cream shop that I really learned the importance of being an honest, hard worker – lessons that serve me well now.

Dad would come into the shop at 3:00 or 4:00 in the morning and work for a few hours making ice cream, and then head to his job at the grocery store. Mom would seemingly be at the shop all day every day. I'd come in after school and on the weekends and work, too.

I got my first "real job" when I was around 16

When I was in high school I worked in a grocery store for a few months – and quickly saw why my Mom wanted to do something other than work in a grocery store! It definitely wasn't for me.

After that I got a job on the weekends that I actually liked: I worked on cars at a car stereo shop, installing stereo systems and alarms in cars. How great is that? I was working with my hands, doing electronics and wiring and all that fun stuff. I guess even at that age I had a natural affinity for this type of work.

Around this time I was blessed with a little sister. She came at a much-needed time for all of us, and I really enjoyed helping to take care of her. I was just 16 and I was changing diapers, having fun playing with her and loving seeing her smile and laugh.

Meanwhile my home life was bad and getting worse

Coming up as a teen, starting when I was maybe 14, things were getting kinda rough at home. Dad's drinking seemed to be increasing and getting worse. With that he got verbally and physically abusive with my brother and me, and would sometimes be that way with Mom, too.

I'll be honest: It was getting ugly. My home life had lots of chaos and craziness. And since by this point in time my parents were not getting along at all (they eventually divorced), things were only getting worse.

Looking back at this as an adult, I forgive my father now, and I can see that he was handed the same deck of cards as his father, who was an abusive drinker, too. I truly believe Dad meant well. He worked *hard*, and he showed me by example that you can have some of the nicer things in life if you're willing to put in the work to get them. But once he started drinking, you never knew what he was going to do.

The chaos really got to me

I don't know how Mom hung in there for as long as she did, but by the time I was 17 I just couldn't take any more of Dad's drunken behavior. So on the last day before winter break I dropped out of school, packed a bag and ran off with a buddy whose home life wasn't any better than mine. Yes, we ran away from home.

I always had miscellaneous jobs. Even so, I wasn't exactly rolling in money. For a while I went from place to place, living on the streets or going couch to couch. Sometimes my friend and I would save up enough to get a little apartment. Then we'd lose the apartment because we couldn't make rent, and the cycle would start again.

I had one heck of a rebellion

Coming out of that chaotic home life I went a bit nuts. I certainly wasn't behaving like the upstanding citizen that I am today, if you know what I mean!

When I was around 18 a friend got me a job in the restaurant industry, where I started as a host and worked my way up to server. From my perspective at the time, there were two great things about working at these restaurants: I only worked evenings, and, thanks to tips, I made a lot more money than I had at the car stereo place. So I could go to work, go partying after work, sleep in and then go back to work to do it all again.

In other words, I had run away from the hurt and chaos of home, just to create a life of more chaos on my own.

Deep down, though, throughout my rebellion years, I was lost. I was hurt. And I was so very, very angry. Although every now and then I talked to my mom, for a few years I pretty much disconnected from my parents. Today, as a parent, I cannot imagine how difficult this must have been for them. Yes, I am sorry Mom. I love you dearly!

Somewhere in there I got my high school diploma

To be honest, I don't remember the exact timing. The reality is, it broke Mom's heart when I dropped out of high school. I considered getting a "GED," which is a high school equivalency diploma. But in Mom's eyes it was better for me to go down the path of getting an actual high school diploma, which is harder. Although I wasn't exactly in close contact with her at the time, to make her happy and to express my love for her I got the diploma.

I missed the challenge of fixing things

Eventually I realized that I wanted to get back to working in the field, that I love things that are more hands on. So I got a job as a mechanic working on jet skis and small personal watercraft. I'd rebuild engines, do the wiring and all the maintenance. Essentially everything mechanical or electrical, I'd do it.

Meanwhile my parents' ice cream shop venture was winding down, and my father and uncle bought an old wrecking yard auto repair shop and turned it into a 4x4 repair shop. Everyone on both sides of my family loves heading out to the desert for off roading, dirt biking and Jeeping in old-school Jeeps, so fixing these vehicles was a natural fit.

By now I was around 21 and Dad asked me to come work for him. This was his way of reaching out to get me off the streets and try to help me, because I was clearly going down a bad path. I'm not sure why, but I accepted his job offer, moved back home and worked at the 4x4 repair shop for about a year.

Mom and Dad wanted something better for me

Dad had a close friend named Bruce who owned a commercial air conditioning shop. I didn't know it, but Dad talked to Bruce about giving me a job. My parents wanted me to have a better career path, and Dad knew that if I learned the HVAC (Heating, Ventilation and Air Conditioning) trade there'd be better pay, training, benefits, etc. For all of his many faults, my father was trying to do right by me.

So he set up a meeting for me with Bruce, and Bruce offered me a job at his commercial air conditioning shop. But there were a few caveats. In order to keep this job I would have to:

- Stop the partying lifestyle and craziness.

- Go to trade school at a local community college that had an excellent two-year HVAC training program. If I screwed up in school they'd fire me.

- Be reliable and dependable.

I fell in love with HVAC

My HVAC career began in August of 1997, when I started school and the job at Bruce's shop at the same time. I worked hard and kept my head down. I was at classes all day Monday and Tuesday, and some evenings. Wednesday through Friday I'd work, plus I'd also try to take any overtime available – both to make extra money and to stay away from the craziness of my parents' house.

For two years I worked my ass off. I gave up the partying lifestyle. It was literally just school, studying, taking tests and working. I went all in on this HVAC thing.

And do you know what? I LOVED it! Even 26 years later I still get excited when I start talking about HVAC! HVAC is a mix of everything I already loved – wiring, electronics, controls, piping, mechanical and more – plus something that was new for me, refrigeration, which is a thermodynamic process. For me it was like, "Wow! I love all of this stuff!" I fell in love with the complexity of everything, the challenge and the fun, and I just poured myself into it.

Although I'm not that great of a student and school had always been hard for me, I ended up being one of the top students in trade school. I guess doing something you love really does make a difference. Plus, it was cool working with a bunch of guys who loved working with their hands doing electrical and mechanical stuff, too.

What really surprised me was the customer service aspect of the business. It's very rewarding being this highly technically-trained mechanic or technician who shows up and saves the day for the hospital or hotel or manufacturing facility or big cold storage warehouse or someone's home. You're a hero! Don't we all want to be heroes?

My business kind of started itself

When I started working as an HVAC technician trainee at the age of 22, I didn't really have a goal or dream. I just thought, "Okay, cool, here's a good job with good pay and benefits. I can make something of myself." It didn't occur to me to dream bigger than that.

Eventually, though, the company I was working for went out of business and laid me off. At the time I had a side job doing some HVAC work for a friend. I figured I'd do side jobs for the summer and then go back to work for another company. But then that first little side job turned into a referral, which turned into another referral, and with the domino effect of referrals before I knew it the work was lined up and never stopped. Once the work started coming I turned it into a business. And here I am 20 years later, running an eight-figure company.

Creating consistent success was a challenge

Making a go of this business is one of the hardest things I've ever done. For a long time it seemed like every time things started to go well, something went wrong. One month we had plenty of work and

I was riding high, and the next month I couldn't pay the bills. It was one heck of a roller coaster.

Then, after many years of trials and tribulations, rags to riches and back again, I finally came to the realization that there was a lot I didn't know about business, leadership, management, systems, structure and more. So I joined an executive coaching group called Vistage, and began what would become my personal and professional development journey.

Eventually I cracked the code

Through many years of getting educated – hiring coaches, reading books, going to seminars, participating in business masterminds, etc. – I started to learn about strategies, tactics and tools to grow my business *and* grow myself personally.

Eventually I cracked the code and saw that all the things I had been studying were interconnected. I began to see clearly that there's a holistic Blueprint for Success that can help you thrive in *all* aspects of life: Your business, health, relationships, mindset, everything.

Today I am living my best life, proof that the Blueprint works. My relationship with my higher power has brought me a completely different perspective regarding my purpose in the world. My wife and I are going strong as a couple. Financially, we're blessed to have a nice house and all the fun things (second home, boat, etc.) that we want. I'm living a healthy lifestyle and feeling better, stronger and more energetic than ever. In addition to my thriving commercial HVAC/R business, I also have a growing coaching business, in which I coach people on how to implement the Blueprint for Success in their lives (see www.BlueCollarKing.com).

I'm writing this book to share the Blueprint for Success with you, so that you won't have to struggle like I did. If you follow it – and I'm warning you now, it won't work if you cut corners – this Blueprint really will show you how to build a life of abundance, fulfillment and results.

If you're ready to start living your best life and willing to put some effort into making it happen, you're going to *love* the Blueprint for Success. Let's get started!

CHAPTER 1:

INTRODUCTION TO THE BLUEPRINT

Abundance, success and fulfillment are all wonderful things. While there were many times in my business' history that I thought I had attained all of this and more, it was always short-lived. I'd get momentum going and we'd be hitting our sales goals, then things would go back down again. We probably had five or six cycles of severe ups and downs.

It wasn't until I learned the concepts behind the Blueprint for Success and started putting these things into action in my personal and business life that everything turned around for good.

Disclosure #1: I didn't invent any of this

Full disclosure: I did not invent the idea of having a system or blueprint for success, and at their core the ideas I am presenting in this book certainly are not original. I'm not saying that they are.

I learned all of this over the course of my own multi-year personal development journey. I tried these ideas out myself and proved to myself that they work. Then I wrapped my head around it all and figured out how to make it more relatable and understandable for people who work in the trades. Then I packaged it into an easy-to-follow "blueprint" format.

Disclosure #2: This is not an "all inclusive" guide

This Blueprint is excellent, and I highly recommend that you read this book, learn the Blueprint and implement it in your life. The ideas, strategies, tactics and tools presented here can certainly hyper-accelerate you in all aspects of your life. However, by no means is this book intended to be the "final answer" all-inclusive guide to life and business. The journey is almost infinite, because there is always more to learn and more to do.

My hope is that you will save yourself a whole lot of time and struggle by beginning here and using the Blueprint for Success as the starting point for your own personal development journey. But there will be more to come!

All of that said, let's dive in.

Here's the big picture

This image represents the Blueprint for Success. Here's how this works…

Pretty much all aspects of your life can be put into one of four categories, which I'm calling the "4 Fs". In the Blueprint these are represented as being like the pillars of a house, because these are the pillars that hold up your life:

1. **Faith** – Your mindset, spirituality, thought processes, religious practices, etc.

2. **Family** – Your personal and professional relationships, including with family and friends

3. **Fitness** – Everything related to how you treat and/or take care of your body

4. **Finance** – How you make money, including how to run your business, and what you do with the money you make

The 4 Fs hold up the "roof," which represents your desired end results of all the good things in life: abundance, success, good health, fulfillment, happiness, joy and more. We will just call this the "Kingdom."

All of this rests on an all-important foundation of *values*, especially the absolute values of truth and integrity. Just like the way a house is only as strong as its foundation, your life is only as strong as its foundation, too. You can do a really good job in all four of these areas of life, but if your truth and integrity are not on a high level, you're building your life on quicksand instead of concrete. Sooner or later, something will give.

All aspects of your life are connected

As I started studying this, one of the things that I found hardest to accept is the idea that all four areas of your life – faith, family, fitness and finance – are connected and equally important. I don't know about you, but I had never seen it this way. "I'm a business owner," I thought. "I need to focus on running my business. There are only so many hours in the day. If that other stuff doesn't happen, oh well, that's how it goes."

So I focused on growing my business (i.e., the "finance" pillar in the Blueprint). And as my business grew, so did my waistline, since I was ignoring fitness. Meanwhile, my relationships suffered. My health took a hit. I was short-tempered. I was taking the "fake it till you make it approach" in business dealings to try to hide my lack of self-confidence. But, hey, I was making money, and that's what counts, right?

Wrong. I learned the hard way that when you focus on just one of the four pillars, the entire structure gets out of balance, the roof slides off and the walls come crashing down.

To be honest, when I was first introduced to mindset, faith, EQ and other similar crap, I thought, "What is this hippy dippy shit? I know what I'm doing in life, I just need a system that I can use to run my business so it will be profitable again." It took me a while to mature in my mindset to understand that all that other stuff – meaning the stuff in the other three pillars – is really what got me messed up. My problem wasn't a flawed business system. It was a flawed approach to life.

Sure, all the business tactics and strategy ideas that I was seeking are all super important. But it was when I started embracing the other three Fs and putting in the work in all four areas of my life that everything holistically lifted up together and things really started going well.

Yes, you need a blueprint

Why should you follow a blueprint? Because without it you're being held back. You wouldn't build a house without a blueprint. You shouldn't build your life without one, either.

Most people don't naturally see their lives objectively. We all have blind spots. As humans – as personal leaders of ourselves and as business leaders – we have patterns in our ways of thinking and of dealing with situations that are holding us back in life, although we are completely blind to them. Having a blueprint gives you a framework through which you can see things objectively and measurably, and possibly even identify your blind spots. It helps you to see what's working and what's not working, so that you can make intelligent decisions about how to go to the next step. What should you improve? What should you keep doing? What should you stop doing?

If you're like most people you're not even asking these questions. You're just showing up. You do the things you think you're supposed to do. And you hope that life, business, God, luck or the universe will bring you the things you need and hope for.

A blueprint lets you take charge of your own destiny and build your success based on a solid foundation and a proven approach.

One of the four pillars is likely to be your weak link

What I've seen is that in these four areas – faith, family, fitness and finance – we all have strengths and weaknesses. Chances are one of them is your "kryptonite," the thing that you tend to avoid at all costs.

The mere thought of doing something, anything, to move ahead in this area scares you. Making progress in this area seems so impossible that you feel defeated before you begin.

Well, I've got news for you, and you're not going to like it. You need to assess this Blueprint, identify your weak pillar and then *lean into it.* Yes, lean into the thing that scares the crap out of you. Doing so is one of the secrets to success with the entire Blueprint.

Why? Because by leaning into your weak pillar you'll build courage, willpower, self-discipline and more. Your level of ability to overcome procrastination and stop listening to the bullshit stories and excuses you tell yourself about why you don't want to do it and shouldn't do it will increase. And no matter how slowly you progress and how long it takes, as you gradually begin to improve, your success with this pillar will transfer to the other three pillars. It will be like rocket fuel propelling you forward in all aspects of your life.

Become a change expert and habit creator

We are all the result of our historical habits and how we have approached life in the past. Where you are today is a result of your past thoughts and behaviors. Which means that if you want to grow and move towards achieving lasting happiness, fulfillment, joy, abundance, etc., you must create new habits.

Using this Blueprint for Success to build this holistic life of freedom and abundance requires you to become a change expert. You must become a master at building the new habits and behaviors that are required to create lasting positive change. Yes, change can be scary. It can also be exciting, when you understand the amazing impact that these changes can have.

The reality is, if you cannot create new habits you have no hope of changing your life for the better. You can read books. You can go to seminars. You can hire a coach or work with a mentor. But if you cannot change, all those things will be a waste of time and money, because you cannot evolve and grow. You'll just remain stuck where you're at. Or, worse, see things in your life go downhill.

It's up to you to do the work

All of this means that you need to learn new ways of thinking and doing things – and that takes work. Are you ready?

Author and motivational speaker Tony Robbins said, "One reason so few of us achieve what we truly want is that we never direct our focus; we never concentrate our power." In this book you will learn what you should direct your focus to in order to achieve the results you want.

Think of your life as being like a construction project. Up until now you were just building randomly, without a plan. Now you have the Blueprint. Like any construction project, however, the devil is in the details of how this Blueprint is implemented … and that's what the rest of this book is about!

Key Points for Chapter 1

- The Blueprint for Success has five parts:

  1. Faith

  2. Family

  3. Fitness

  4. Finance

  5. Foundation

- All aspects of your life are connected, so all aspects of the Blueprint are important.

- Following this Blueprint makes it much easier to move ahead in life.

- You need to become an expert at creating new habits and behaviors.

Chapter 1 Exercise

Study the Blueprint for Success diagram and give yourself some honest feedback regarding which of the 5 areas (Faith, Family, Fitness, Finance, Foundation) have been getting short shrift in your life.

CHAPTER 2:

BUILDING
THE FOUNDATION

Just like a house or an office tower, the four pillars of life (i.e., the "4 Fs," Faith, Family, Fitness and Finance) must be supported. In order to last, everything must stand on a strong foundation. While your house stands on concrete, your life needs to stand on a strong foundation of *values*.

I've broken these down into *absolute values*, which are universal, and *core values*, which are specific to you, your family, your company or other group.

Absolute values

In the strong foundation of the Blueprint for Success, **truth and integrity** are the absolute values that every person or group needs to have. But when it comes to building a foundation for your life, what do "truth" and "integrity" really mean?

Truth is simple. Don't lie. Never, ever lie about anything, because you won't achieve true and lasting success if you're a person who lies.

The result of truth is being a person of integrity. It's about operating with a belief and mindset that your word is your law. Integrity means keeping the promises and commitments that you make to yourself and others.

If you say, "I'll do such-and-such by tomorrow evening," this means that you are committing to doing everything in your power to get that thing done by tomorrow evening. Otherwise, your statement was a lie – especially if you did not even make an attempt to get the thing done. If it doesn't happen, you were not being truthful. You lied and you failed to act with integrity. This is the case whether or not you explicitly said, "I promise." If you say you'll do something, you are making a commitment, and you need to follow through.

If truth and integrity are not in place in your life, the rest of the Blueprint is not effective or sustainable.

You must have truth and integrity with yourself

One of the many reasons that truth and integrity are so important is that self-confidence comes from having truth and integrity with yourself. Self-confidence, in turn, gives you power and strength.

You might think that self-confidence comes from repeatedly doing a task well, or from getting praise from others. Actually, at its core, self-confidence comes from living a life of truth and integrity.

Are you keeping the promises and commitments that you make to yourself? If you tell yourself that you'll do something, even if it's something seemingly trivial such as turning off the TV after one more episode of a show, do you keep this promise?

Here's something about how your mind works. If you repeatedly break the promises and commitments that you make to yourself, then your subconscious mind will know that it cannot trust you. When this happens, you will basically be in conflict with yourself. You'll tell yourself you're going to do something, but you won't believe yourself. In other words, you won't have confidence in yourself. That's why this conflict will manifest as a lack of self-confidence. After all, how can you have self-confidence if, deep down, you don't even trust yourself to do what you say you will do?

Often when you see people in life who are overly hesitant and afraid to take action, this is their real problem. At the psychological level they just don't trust themselves, so they don't have the self-confidence to make a decision.

This is why, first and foremost, acting with truth and integrity starts with the promises and commitments that you make to yourself. The key to developing the habit of keeping these promises and commitments is to start small.

Start with little things, get in the habit of keeping these promises, and gradually build trust with yourself. It's like going to the gym. If you haven't been to the gym in five years, you're not going to start by bench pressing 200 pounds on day one. Instead you'll start with lighter weights, get in shape, and work your way up. When you're building a new mindset around the absolute values of truth and integrity, it's like getting your mind in shape. And the way to start down this path is with small new habits.

You must have truth and integrity with others

So you start internally, because that's where you can most easily build from. As always acting with truth and integrity becomes a habit, your self-confidence will grow and you'll start approaching life from a place of greater strength. All of this will start to show. Your energy will change. You will exude a sense of confidence and dependability, and others will start to perceive you differently.

When you are a person of truth and integrity, people will actually feel it in the energy around you. They will be more drawn to you and more likely to feel comfortable around you. The opposite is also true. Ever meet someone who just seemed "slimy" and untrustworthy, even before they spoke? Maybe you walked by somebody at the store and your internal radar immediately told you to keep an eye out. Chances are they were not a person of truth and integrity, and you felt it.

Of course, truth and integrity must be both internal and external. It's not enough to keep the promises that you make to yourself. You must also be truthful with and keep the promises that you make to others, too. The Blueprint doesn't work if you fully trust yourself but you're not a reliable person externally.

That said, what happens if you make a commitment that you later realize you cannot keep? After all, you're human and stuff happens. Although your follow-through will never be 100%, you *can* be 100% with *communicating* about your commitments.

If you can't deliver, always let the affected person know as soon as you realize you can't deliver. Don't just blow it off and apologize later. Or, even worse, blow it off and then never mention it again, pretending that you never made the commitment in the first place!

Be a person of declaration and commitment

A key point here is that truth and integrity must be absolute, not selective. If you want to achieve lasting success you can't have selective integrity, or integrity only when it's convenient. You can't be truthful only in certain circumstances. Acting this way will negate your power and energy.

Instead of being a person of wishes and hopes, be a person of declaration and commitment. When you say you'll do something, do it – whether or not it's convenient, and even if you must prioritize this commitment over doing something else that you'd rather do. If you tell your spouse that you will build a new deck by the end of the month, you need to make building a new deck a higher priority than sitting back with a beer and watching the big game on TV.

Be results-driven, not excuse-driven. Don't be a sugar coater, either. It seems like it's almost like an addiction for some people. They say they'll do something, then they struggle to follow through with the commitment. So they start telling "little white lies" and giving little excuses and sugar coating the real reasons why the thing isn't getting done. They hunt for every reason or validation as to why the fact that they've broken their promise should be perfectly acceptable to the other person. And this behavior only tends to get worse and worse over time.

The selective integrity or sugarcoating path is a slippery slope that leads to you being a slippery person who is not dependable.

Here's what I personally learned when I stopped telling a little lie here and a little bullshit excuse there and started living a life of greater truth and integrity instead. The cleaner I got with myself and others, the better I felt about myself. People started to depend on me and trust me, and I started to trust myself. My self-confidence grew. I began to have more energy with the world. Things got better.

The bottom line is, you can either deliver and produce results, or you can make excuses. You can't do both. Acting with truth and integrity builds your self-confidence. It gives you power, strength and honor. It's foundational.

Core values

Okay, so if the absolute values in the foundation of the Blueprint for Success are the universal values of truth and integrity, what are the core values? Well, that's for you to decide. Core values are not universal. They're variable and specific to a person or group's character.

Core values are words and statements that give you guidelines as to how you should act, think and behave in order to achieve beneficial and empowering results. They're tools that help drive how you live your life within the Blueprint for Success framework.

Having a clearly defined set of core values helps you make the right decisions, which then produce the right behaviors, which then produce the desired results.

For a group of people, such as a family or a company, having a shared set of core values that everyone agrees upon gets everyone into alignment as you work together towards a shared goal. Core values also help define what matters most to you as an individual or to a group to which you belong. What is it that you cherish most?

How to define your core values

The system that I recommend is based on using a deck of "values cards." Each card in the deck lists a different value, such as "Adventure," "Joy," or "Grit." You can find a selection of these online at Amazon.com.

Here's how to define your personal core values:

1. Buy a deck of values cards.

2. Go through all the cards in the deck and pick out 25 words that most resonate with you and your beliefs, characters and goals.

3. Look at these cards once every day or two for about a week, and then narrow it down to 12 or 13 cards.

4. Repeat this process until you have narrowed it down to the five to seven values that matter most to you.

Note that you really do need to allow time for this process. It's not just a one-hour thing, as you need to carefully consider your choices to be sure they truly are representative of what you believe matters most.

If you're working with a group, the process is very similar:

1. Each person gets their own deck of value cards.

2. Each person goes through all the cards in the deck and picks out 25 words that most resonate with them as being important values for the group to have.

3. Everyone puts their 25 cards on the table and you see which ones were chosen by multiple people. These get set aside in a "possibilities" pile.

4. Everyone takes a week and narrows down what they've got left by 50%.

5. Repeat this process a few times.

6. Revisit the cards in the "possibilities" pile and, as a group, narrow it down to the final five to seven values. This might take some

discussion and negotiation. Also, sometimes it just comes down to choosing between two different words that essentially represent the same behavior. In this case you can simply take a vote and choose one.

Once everyone creates these values together and you all agree upon them, you're in sync. Now it's a matter of using these core values to guide your decisions and behavior. You might get off track here and there, but the core values are the guidelines or map that remind you which way you want to go. When you get off track you look to your core values to guide you.

Your core values will reflect what matters most to *you*.

Key Points for Chapter 2

- Your life needs to stand on a strong foundation of *values*.

- Every person or group needs to have the *absolute values* of truth and integrity.

- You need to have truth and integrity with both yourself and others.

- Your *core values* are unique to you or your group. Defining them and then keeping them front and center will help you make the right decisions in life.

Chapter 2 Exercise

Order a deck of values cards and follow the steps outlined above to identify your personal core values.

CHAPTER 3:

UNDERSTANDING THE FAITH PILLAR,
PART 1 — FAITH & SPIRITUALITY

In the Blueprint for Success, the Faith pillar is not just about what you may think of as "religion." It's much broader than that. In addition to religion or faith, it also includes your mindset, spirituality and thoughts, as well as self-care practices related to building a stronger mindset. As you will soon understand, all these thing are interrelated.

In this chapter we'll delve into the faith and spirituality aspects of this pillar.

Faith is believing in something bigger than us

Connecting to a force or power that is greater than your own conscious self is a super power. Unlocking your potential starts with believing in something that is greater than yourself.

Some people believe in the Universe and its energy, vibrations and powers. Others believe that there is a higher level of consciousness that they can tap into that resides inside their minds. Many connect with the belief systems of specific religious groups, such as Christianity, Buddhism, Judaism, Islam or Hinduism.

I'm not here to preach. Whatever form your faith takes is beautiful. But I do feel strongly that everyone needs to find something to connect to in the spirit of faith, whether that is a higher level of consciousness that is found inside of you or a higher power that resides outside of you. Without this connection, your capabilities and the results you'll see everywhere in your life will be capped.

Regardless of what spirit you believe in, you are a spiritual creature. In fact, as I have come to understand, we are all spiritual creatures having a human experience – not vice versa. Once you lean into that and embrace it, you may be surprised by how much this impacts other areas of your life.

Faith can give you mental strength

As you have undoubtedly experienced, there are always two different energies or forces that pull on us as humans. Good and bad. Right and wrong. Yin and yang. Whatever you call it, these forces are not just "out there" outside of your being. They also connect to your internal voice, the little voice in your head that sometimes seems to be constantly talking.

Have you ever seen one of those cartoons where someone has a little devil sitting on one shoulder and a little angel sitting on the other, and the two are trying to pull the person in opposite directions? That's a great way to picture how these two forces in the universe can mess with your head and your life.

One of the reasons I say that faith gives you mental strength has to do with how you deal with these two opposing forces. When you have a spiritual connection to something greater than yourself, this helps you to tap in more to the force for good in the universe. And it helps you defend against the attacks from the force for bad in the universe.

Having this spiritual connection will therefore help you make better decisions, even if the better or right decision is not the thing that you really want to do. For example, when the negative force is urging you to spend money unnecessarily on things that really don't matter in the long run, and giving you all kinds of excuses for doing this, the positive force is reminding you that you should use that money for more important things.

Having faith in a higher force fuels your ability to resist temptations and make the right decisions more often.

Faith can change how you see things

I have also seen that faith can help you see the things that happen in your life in a different context or perspective.

It seems like for many of us, our default mental setting is negative. We think in terms of things happening *to* us, categorize every event in our lives as either "good" or "bad," and get stuck in a victim mindset when something is "bad."

For example, say you get into a car accident. Someone T-bones you in an intersection on your way home from work. No one is hurt, but your car is a mess.

If you're like most people, a whole load of negative thoughts will start swimming in your head. "Wow, I can't believe I got into an accident!" "This is horrible!" "Why did this have to happen to *me*?" And so forth.

Here's a mind-blowing idea that I struggled with for a long time: *Reacting this way is a choice*, and you can choose to react differently. When an event happens, that negative force will be working hard to get you to only see the problem. What is the positive force trying to tell you?

What if everything that happens is just an event, with no "good or bad" concept attached to it? What if everything happens for a reason, if we choose to find the lesson?

Personally, as I've grown in my own spirituality, I've created a new lens through which I see the world. The more connected I get, the more I see each event or circumstance in my life without a "good or bad" rating, but just as something that is happening.

I now see that everything in life is not "good" or "bad." It's just the way the world works. But *everything teaches us*. There is a lesson inside every event that happens to you. It's up to you to build the filter/lens/spirit/mindset to see what that event is trying to teach you.

Being connected to a higher power gives me rocket fuel to connect to life's lessons. It helps me get out of the victim mindset and gives me tools and power to fight through difficult times. It can do the same for you.

Faith can help you change your approach to challenges

The more you lean into your faith and higher power, the more you'll be able to trust that there's a plan. The more you trust that there's a plan, the easier it is to be patient when you face a challenge, and not just try to *control and fix things now*. Because that negative force in the universe wants to push you to do everything *right now* – to act rashly, before you've had a chance to think about it.

When you need to resolve a problem with your business, or have a tough conversation with your spouse or co-worker, or deal with some other issue, the universe's negative forces want you to fight for immediate results. But that "immediate fix and control" approach almost always produces undesirable results, especially if you're dealing with another person. No one wants to be "fixed and controlled" by someone else!

Instead, seek to provide more space to think and let your higher power show you how to accomplish your goal. When you lean into that, you're leaning into the universe's positive forces and rejecting the negative. It's a better approach to dealing with life's challenges, and it produces better results.

Faith can give you more confidence

All of these things associated with faith and spirituality – having greater mental strength, seeing things differently, changing your approach to challenges and more – can play an important part in giving you more confidence.

When you tap into a higher power, you begin to walk the world with an understanding that the negative forces and energies in the world don't have power over you. As a result, you begin to experience an internal sense of safety. You feel more secure about yourself and what you are capable of. In other words, you feel more confident.

In the men's group that I belong to we talk about something called "Godfidence." There's something good that seems to happen energetically and spiritually to people who lean into the positive forces of the world. I can see this in others who walk the world with a beautiful energy and confidence about them. This is something that you can experience, too.

Faith is often the missing piece

On January 7, 2022, I met my friend Steve Weatherford. The way he talked about the importance of faith in his life really resonated for me. In fact, thanks to Steve, something in me shifted that day. I don't know what it was, but there was something about Steve's speech, energy, story and truths that planted a seed for faith in me.

Back in the day, Steve was a punter in the NFL. He was physically fit, made lots of money and was living an enviable life of fame and glamour. But something felt wrong and his life felt unfulfilling. He wasn't connecting to lasting abundance, happiness and joy. Everything was fleeting.

Then, he explained to me, he finally figured out what was missing. "I had a God hole," he said. Steve was doing the work in 3 of the 4 F's, but the Faith pillar was laying on the ground.

It was the same for me.

Many people are resistant to faith

For most of my life I was a "Christmas tree" Christian. My connection to Christianity started and ended with my family's celebration of Christmas as an excuse to give and receive gifts. I didn't believe in God. I didn't feel connected to a higher power. And I didn't give much thought to any of this.

Then I went to that event at which I met my friend Steve. It was a men's gathering in Texas that took place after an amazing business mastermind event. I found myself in a roomful of very successful guys, including doctors, lawyers and other professionals. There were men who owned hundreds of buildings and men who were multi-millionaires.

The more I talked to the people at this gathering, including Steve, the more I saw that they all seemed to have the same things. Not just success, but true fulfillment. A sense of purpose, a deep confidence, a desire to do good in the world. Not coincidentally, some of these men attended the same church and had a strong connection to a higher power.

Like many, I had always been resistant to the idea of connecting with a higher power, probably because I thought it wasn't "cool." Spirituality just isn't flashy or popular. I had always hung around with groups of people who were not religious. My friends weren't into church – they were into partying, boats, off roading, money and fast cars. I thought that was all the "cool" stuff, so I wanted it too.

Back then I thought that people who are religious are soft, docile creatures who hide in the corner. I thought that being religious meant you had to be so humble that you couldn't make money, speak your truth or be bold. So I thought you couldn't be cool and be religious or spiritual. I didn't think you could be a strong masculine force for good on the planet and also be a believer.

Hanging out in a room full of bold, ridiculously successful people who were also men of faith, I realized I was wrong. And I realized that, like Steve, I also had a "God hole."

Today I am practicing Christianity and continuing to work on my spirituality daily. I have a strong belief in a higher power. I believe in living life with a biblical world view and having that mindset in everything I do. Today my life is not just about building results; it's also about giving back.

Once I filled my "God hole" and stepped into my faith at a higher level, it was amazing to me how everything in life started to make more sense and work better. I don't want to sound too out there, but it was literally a revelation and paradigm shift for me. I no longer felt lost or unfulfilled. After being on a continuous pursuit of personal growth for many years, I saw that this was the final piece of the puzzle.

So does this mean I think that *you* need to be or become a Christian in order to follow the Blueprint for Success? No, not at all. As I said earlier, I'm not here to preach. Whatever form your faith takes is beautiful. What I do think is important is that you need to believe in a higher power. The form that this belief takes for you does not have to be the same as the form it takes for me.

In fact, there's no reason for you to jump into a particular religion or spiritual practice. Look into or try different spiritual practices and beliefs. Do some research. Talk to others, pray, meditate, explore and see what resonates and feels right to you.

Key Points for Chapter 3

- The Faith pillar of the Blueprint for Success is not just about "religion." It also includes your mindset, spirituality and thoughts.

- Faith is believing in something bigger than us.

- Faith can make a huge difference in your life in many areas, including your mental strength, viewpoint, confidence and approach to challenges.

Chapter 3 Exercise

You don't have to take my word for any of this stuff about believing in a higher power. Instead, try it out for yourself. For the next 3, 6 or 12 months, lean into it as a possibility. Take down your internal barriers, give it a try and then evaluate the results.

CHAPTER 4:

UNDERSTANDING THE FAITH PILLAR,
PART 2 – MINDSET & EMOTIONAL INTELLIGENCE

"EQ" or "Emotional Quotient" is another word for your "emotional intelligence." Mindset and EQ are both important parts of the Faith pillar. "Mindset" means your mental attitude, outlook and thought patterns. It's the way that you always tend to think about or react to things.

Two important aspects of your mindset are your level of "grit" (i.e., mental toughness) and your level of self-discipline. I see grit as the ability to do the right thing *in the moment* – to do what is needed or required – even when your body and willpower are saying "I don't want to!" Self-discipline, on the other hand, is more about a long-haul commitment to consistently and sustainably doing the right thing. Grit helps you successfully deal with the unexpected issues that pop up. Self-discipline gets you to the gym every morning.

Emotional intelligence is basically your ability to be aware of, control and express your emotions *in a positive way*. People with a high EQ are often more successful in life. They're self-aware. They control their impulsive feelings and behaviors. They have empathy and get along well with others.

Your mindset and EQ are often tied together. Both impact your thoughts, which, as I'll explain in the next chapter, have a big impact on the results you get in life. And just like faith, your mindset and EQ are things that you can change.

In fact, for the Blueprint for Success to work, you must be willing to change. You must develop an abundance-based growth mindset. You must have the attitude that you are committed to growth, and committed to being open to new perspectives, possibilities and ways of being and learning new tools that at first might not seem possible.

Leaders must have a high level of grit and self-discipline

If you want to build a business, be a leader in your family or community, and/or do anything to improve your life, you must have a high level of mental toughness and grit. You must have the ability to "struggle well," because the good things that you want in your life are not likely to come easy.

People who are what I call "gritty" tend to see and find opportunity and lessons in life's challenges. They have learned to "dance in the rain," because they understand not all storms come to disrupt their strategies, processes or goals. Some storms come to clear the path.

Some of the most successful leaders I know have an extremely high level of grit. They're not thrown off guard by breakdowns, issues or problems. Sure, they might get temporarily emotionally triggered or upset by these things. But then they quickly recover, get back in the game and start solving the problems. Ultimately a leader's job is to deliver results and fix issues. If you don't have the grit to do that, you will fail as a leader.

In contrast, people who lack grit and mental toughness tend to break easily. When faced with a challenge they quickly give up. "It's too hard!" they'll complain. "I'm not meant for this!" they'll whine. Their victim-based mindset and attitude stops them from moving ahead.

People who have a high level of grit also have self-discipline, which, like I said before, is like the "gas" that keeps you going over the long haul, sustaining you in consistently doing the things you need to do, whether or not these things are enjoyable or easy.

Having self-discipline does not mean that you'll never get off track with the good habits and practices you are establishing in your personal and professional life. But it does mean that more often than not you'll stay the course, and if you do get off track, that detour will be short-lived.

EQ is often linked to childhood experiences

What was your childhood like? The way that you respond to events and people today – in other words, your current EQ – is probably linked to your very early childhood. Your childhood experiences probably influenced your current mindset, too.

Here's why. From birth until around age seven your brain was evolving very quickly. One of the things it was doing was building a "roadmap" of how to interact with others and the world in general. Since you didn't know differently, this roadmap was based on the environment you and your developing brain found yourself in.

If you were lucky you came from a loving, caring, nurturing family led by stable adults. You always felt safe and loved. You learned positive ways to interact with the world, and that's serving you well now.

If you were unlucky you had a traumatic childhood. You didn't always feel safe and loved. Unless you've done the work to move past this, the lessons you learned are not serving you well now.

A traumatic childhood has a lasting impact

Say you were one of the unlucky ones. Maybe you were in a home filled with verbal or physical abuse, screaming, cussing and hitting. Maybe your parents were alcoholics or drug addicts. Whatever the details, it was a lot of chaos and unpredictability – and that was a very stressful and traumatic environment for little you. Just when your brain was in its most important time of development, you were living in a state of fear and uncertainty.

Unlike that lucky kid who grew up in the loving household, you did *not* learn positive ways to interact with the world. In fact, your young brain didn't know what to do with all that trauma, so it created defense mechanisms. It started building a "survival mindset" long before you were ready for such a thing.

Here's a question for you. Are you an easily-triggered "hot head"? I often hear people say, "I have a very short fuse. I've always been like that. God made me that way."

I used to be one of the biggest hot heads on the planet! Every little thing triggered me, and it seemed like I was frequently angry. But now I've learned something important: God didn't make me that way. He didn't make you that way, either. We were all made with all the tools we need to have a high level of emotional control (i.e., a high EQ).

When you were growing up you learned what discomfort is and what it feels like to be physically or emotionally hurt. Each time you experienced something scary or hurtful, little reference points were created in your brain that told your brain these things are scary and bad and can hurt you.

Unfortunately, if early on in life you were exposed to uncertainty, trauma and chaos, especially if this happened over and over again, this created a lot of these reference points that make it easier for things that happen to you now to trigger a response that's really all about things that happened to you back then. Specifically, your childhood trauma can cause the "fight or flight" response in you now.

Here's why…

For your safety, your subconscious mind is always scanning the horizon looking for threats. When you encounter events or situations, your brain looks at these things and checks to see if they seem similar to anything that hurt or scared you in the past, took you out of your comfort zone or may have even been a life or death situation. If the answer is yes, your subconscious mind will essentially scream, "Danger! Danger!" At this point your "fight or flight" response will be activated and you will have a visceral, emotional reaction to what is going on. You will be triggered.

You will also relive the emotions you felt way back when the event that created that reference point in your brain took place. Instead of reacting to what's happening now, you end up reacting to what happened then.

However, chances are whatever triggered you now is not a life-threatening situation. It may not even be an actual danger. But because your brain thinks it looks similar to something frightening or upsetting from your childhood, suddenly your body goes into this state where it puts all its resources into dealing with danger. You might get massive surges of two hormones, adrenaline and cortisol. You can quickly get into a highly emotional response. You're furious. You're so frustrated you want to scream. You just want to shut down and get away from the people who triggered you. Whatever. It's not good.

And the more you were exposed to trauma as a child, the easier it is for you to get triggered like this now.

Other childhood lessons
can also cause problems for you

What happens with a lot of parents is they're busy. They're trying to relax or get dinner made or catch up on some work or whatever. Meanwhile their kid is nagging them for something. Mom? Mom? Mom? Mom? Please, can I have it? Please? Please? Please?

Mom might manage to keep saying no for a while. But eventually the kid goes into a fit of rage and throws a temper tantrum, and Mom gives in so she can get back to what she was doing. Unfortunately, this teaches the child that their anger is a useful tool that they can use to get what they want. The more often this happens, the more the behavior is reinforced, and the more quickly that anger comes on.

If this happened in your childhood, you may wonder why you immediately get so furious at every little thing that bugs you. And you might not understand that your sudden rage will also trigger a fight-or-flight response that makes you behave inappropriately.

For example, say your boss tells you something you don't like. You get super emotionally triggered and then try to use rage and anger to argue with your boss in order to get what you want. But you're an adult now, and the work world doesn't operate that way. Behave like this a few times and instead of getting your way you may get fired. Or behave like this too much as a boss and the employees might quit.

Key Points for Chapter 4

- *Mindset* means your mental attitude, outlook and thought patterns.

- Two important aspects of your mindset are your level of "grit" (i.e., mental toughness) and your level of self-discipline.

- *EQ* or *Emotional Quotient* is about your ability to be aware of, control and express your emotions in a positive way.

- Your childhood likely had a big impact on your mindset and EQ as an adult.

Chapter 4 Exercise

Spend some time thinking about your current level of emotional intelligence. How well do you respond to the things that happen in life? Are you easily triggered or are you even keeled? Are you a hot head who pushes people away with your angry outbursts? Do you shut down, stop communicating and give people the cold shoulder when they piss you off? Are you an empathetic person who gets along well with others? And so forth.

Then think about your childhood. What kind of environment did you grow up in? What core beliefs did you pick up? How might these things be affecting how you respond to life now?

If you realize that you've got a problem, commit to taking action to change things.

CHAPTER 5:

UNDERSTANDING THE FAITH PILLAR,
PART 3 — BRAIN FUNCTION & THOUGHTS

When I first started learning about all this mindset stuff, the things I learned about the brain, and the impact that your thoughts have on your outcomes, blew me away. Like most people I didn't really know anything about how the brain functions … and I didn't think it was something I needed to know. And as far as thoughts are concerned, I assumed that they "just happen." I had no idea that my thoughts were something I could have some mastery over, or that they had anything to do with the results I was seeing in my life.

Now I know better. And after you read this chapter, you'll know better, too.

You've got a lizard brain and a wizard brain

There's this idea about your brain that you need to understand:

- **Your "wizard brain"** is all the parts of your brain where you have access to love, empathy, joy, creation, complex thought, impulse control and more. It's your authentic state.

- **Your "lizard brain"** is the part of your brain that is responsible for dealing with threats and managing your safety.

When you are in that fight-or-flight response, and all that adrenaline and cortisol is rushing through your system, you are in lizard brain mode. You are hopped up on hormones and acting mostly on instinct. You are ready to deal with the threat – to run for your life, dash into the burning building to save your loved ones, etc. In other words, you are ready to have a fight or flight response.

What you are not ready to do, in fact not even capable of doing, is think straight. Because when you are in your lizard brain you cannot access your wizard brain. Which means that when you're in that highly triggered state you don't have access to higher-level resources to resolve the situation in any way other than fight or flight.

It's when you're in your lizard brain that you are most likely to say and do things that you will later regret. What type of things? Well, some people quit their jobs when they're in that lizard brain state. Some fight with their spouse or hit their children. Some get into brawls and end up in jail. Some people simply make very quick, unintelligent decisions. It's often not pretty.

It is not until you are able to leave the situation (mentally, physically or both) that your body calms down, the hormonal surge ends and you are able to go from lizard to wizard. Often what happens is when you go to sleep that night your nervous system and mindset reset during the night and you wake up in wizard brain, your authentic self.

That, of course, is when the feelings of regret set in. You didn't mean to say that nasty thing or do that terrible thing. You feel bad. You feel dumb. If you got into a fight with someone, you may even realize the other person was right. Or it might not be until later that you find out that your lizard brain made a big decision or change that turned out to be a bad one.

Luckily there are some tools that can help you overcome this problem. I'll get into these in the next chapter.

Even minor issues can send you into your "lizard brain"

Triggers and responses come in all shapes and sizes. Some triggered states are big and dramatic. You're red-hot furious! Others are much more subtle. What you feel is more like a slight irritation, such as a little anxiety, discomfort, frustration, disappointment or nervousness. Or your reaction might be somewhere in between these two extremes.

You might externalize your reaction to a trigger or you might internalize it. You might lash out at others, yelling, snapping, etc. Or you might retreat into a quiet mode where you don't respond or communicate at all.

The thing to know is that even in a "minor" triggered state you are still in your "lizard brain," without access to your "wizard brain." The art of the game in taking command of your EQ is to notice these feelings in real time, acknowledge that you are triggered and be mindful of the fact that you may not be seeing things clearly at that moment.

Your brain doesn't like change

Here's another thing you need to understand about your brain. One of the reasons why growth and change can be so difficult is that change basically goes against your natural inclination as a human. For the sake of your survival, at the core level your brain is built to keep you safe. Deep down you do not like change, since change can be dangerous. By default you only want to believe what you already believe, because if you are already right there's no reason to change ... and change can be dangerous. Danger is not "safe."

Because of this, all human brains have what's called "confirmation bias." This means that as you take in new information, your brain will work hard to find a way to use this information to simply confirm what you already believe. It will resist seeing that this new information shows that your current beliefs may be flawed.

At the subconscious level, your brain only wants you to see what you already believe to be true and what you already believe you are capable of. Your brain has what is called the Reticular Activating System (RAS), which acts as a filter to make sense of the millions of bits of information that your eyes and ears and the rest of your body take in every second. Your RAS will constantly look for things that align with your beliefs, and filter out things that do not.

Where does your subconscious mind get its beliefs? From your thoughts.

What happens if you're constantly telling yourself that you're not enough, thinking about how upset you are that others have things that you don't, taking the victim mindset and so forth? Or if you keep thinking that growing your business is not possible, being a leader is too hard, etc.? Your subconscious mind will believe you and your RAS will look for ways to confirm these beliefs.

Your thoughts create your reality

Your mind is incredibly powerful, and the power of thought goes far beyond what you may have imagined.

There is an excellent and very short book that I highly recommend, "As a Man Thinketh," by James Allen. If you buy the book, be sure to get the "21st century" edition. The original was written in 1903, and the new edition rephrases things in more modern language.

In this book, James Allen explains that what you think is what you become. In this sense you are literally what you think. This is because:

Thoughts → Emotions → Behavior → Results

- Your thoughts impact your emotions.

- Your emotions generate your behavior.

- Your behavior produces your results.

Your brain is always trying to prove itself correct. What you tell yourself is what you will come to believe. Your body will then act on this belief and make it happen. In this way your thoughts can become self-fulfilling prophecies.

So, for example, say you're a technician. If you are constantly telling yourself that your boss is out to screw you – if you keep having that thought over and over and over again – you will begin to believe it. You won't even notice anything your boss does that shows he's really not out to screw you, because your brain wants to prove itself correct.

Instead you'll keep thinking, "He's out to screw me." You'll complain to your buddies, "Man, I can't do anything right. My boss is just out to screw me." This, of course, will make you feel and act angry and bitter at work … which will impact your performance … which will cause you to get a negative performance review … which will reinforce your belief that your boss is out to screw you. What you won't see is how your own thoughts and behaviors caused this. You'll insist that it's all because your boss is a jerk.

But this works the other way, too. What if you believe that there's opportunity all around you? What if you tell yourself how great it is to have a job with so many opportunities to learn and grow? Instead of complaining, you talk about the positive things happening at work. In this case your positive thoughts will lead to positive emotions and a different set of behaviors. You'll feel optimistic. You'll come to work with a positive attitude and put in the extra effort to do an excellent job. You'll seek out opportunities to improve your skills. Not surprisingly, you'll be the first one on management's mind when they're looking for someone to promote.

The same concept applies in running a business. If you tell yourself enough times things like, "It's too hard," "I can't grow," "I don't have the ability to be a good leader," "This is impossible," "I'm set up to fail," etc., etc., you'll start to believe that these statements are true. Then you'll start to manifest these things and make it all become a reality. But if you tell yourself the opposite, that you truly are capable of success, then success is what you will start to believe and manifest.

Another way to look at all this is through what's known as the Law of Attraction. The Law of Attraction is based on the fact that at the molecular level, everything is energy – and like attracts like. Your thoughts and mindset have a certain energy. If they are positive, this will attract positive things. If they are negative, this will attract negative things. We attract what we are, and we are what we think.

The example that James Allen gives is to imagine that your mind is like a garden. You are the gardener, and you get to choose what seeds you plant in this garden. If you plant beautiful flowers you will get beautiful flowers. If you plant ugly weeds, you will get ugly weeds. What are these "seeds" that you are planting in your mind? Your thoughts!

If you're always thinking negative or unhelpful thoughts, it's like you're going into your garden and planting weeds. Those negative thoughts will lead to you feeling unhappy/incapable/defeated/unworthy/etc. Because your behavior will then come from this place of negative emotions, your behavior is likely to be negative, too. All of this will work together to produce results that you won't be happy with.

You can also reverse engineer this. If you see that you have a lot of things in your life that are not going well, you can see this as a sign that you must have planted weeds. You need to fix your thinking (pull the weeds and plant something else instead), because your thoughts ultimately create your results.

Many of your thoughts come from your deep-rooted beliefs

Unless you've been working to change this, the environment in which you grew up is having a huge impact on your thoughts today. This is because you have deep-rooted beliefs – that you might not even be consciously aware of – that you picked up during your childhood from your family, teachers, "tribe" or society.

For example, say you were raised in a very poor family. Your parents struggled to put food on the table and a roof over your head. Their mindset, which they may or may not have said out loud, was that this was just the way things are. "We need to be humble." "We're just not the type of people who have been gifted by the universe with money."

"We don't deserve to have a lot of money." "It's impossible for us to ever get ahead." They may have even thought that money is bad. "Money is the root of all evil."

Where did your parents get these core beliefs? Most likely from their parents! Until someone decides to change their beliefs and stop the pattern, core beliefs are usually passed down the generations.

If that's the environment you were raised in, you now have a deep-rooted core belief that there's something bad about money. You think that you don't deserve to have money, you're always going to struggle financially, you're not capable of making money and so forth. These beliefs show up in your thoughts.

What happens if you actually get to a place where you start to make money? Your subconscious brain will work hard to get your reality to align with this core belief and these thoughts, and you'll start self-sabotaging your success. You'll do things that will destroy all of this abundance.

Yes, this sucks. It's horrible. I have experienced this myself. But I'm telling you that if you don't do something to change this dynamic (which you'll learn about in the next chapter), this is what happens.

On the other hand, maybe you were fortunate to be born into a family that has a few generations of leadership. Your family has plenty of money. They're spiritual people who believe strongly in giving back. You were raised in an environment of abundance, fulfillment and generosity. You were shown how to be a strong leader. You learned systems and processes. You saw and internalized the ideas that you will be successful in life, make a good living and know what to do with the money you make so that it will be a source of good.

In this situation you have a very, very high likelihood of becoming a leader and creating a life of prosperity, abundance and fulfillment. You have a deep-rooted core belief that you deserve this and are capable of creating it. Your brain actively pushes you in the right direction to make the right decisions, so that this belief can manifest as your reality.

To change your life you must change your thoughts

Since your thoughts impact your emotions, which generate your behavior, which produces your results, it stands to reason that the only way to change your results is to change your thoughts.

Did you know that your brain runs transient patterns of thought? Thoughts are coming and going all the time. While you can't necessarily control exactly what thoughts show up, you *do* have command over what you do with your thoughts. With training and practice (which we'll get into in the next chapter), you can learn to become aware of your thoughts and "hit the brakes" on those that are not serving you well. Then you can learn to *shift* your thoughts from negative to positive, from unhelpful to helpful.

This is what peak performers do. Studies have shown that one of the things that peak performers and highly effective leaders have in common is that they are able to take command over their thoughts and stop the negative patterns before they take over.

When events happen, unless it's something amazing such as winning the lottery, people tend to immediately have a negative bias around it. That's just how we're wired as humans. We experience most events as irritations. Our thoughts, emotions and reactions are negative. We complain. We get into that negative, victim mindset. Woe is me.

The peak performers don't do that.

Key Points for Chapter 5

- Your "wizard brain" gives you access to love, complex thought, impulse control and more, while your "lizard brain" deals with threats when you're in "fight-or-flight" mode. You cannot access both of these parts of your brain at the same time.

- Your thoughts create your reality: Thoughts → Emotions → Behavior → Results.

- To change your life you must change your thoughts.

Chapter 5 Exercise

For the next three days, pay attention to your thoughts and try to notice when they are negative. Every time you catch yourself having a thought about something that you do not actually want, such as "I'm fat" or "My spouse annoys the heck out of me" or "We'll never hit our sales goals," say to yourself, "Oops, there's another one." The idea here is not to start kicking yourself for having these thoughts. This is just to start building awareness of what's going on in your head.

CHAPTER 6:

IMPLEMENTING THE PRINCIPLES OF THE FAITH PILLAR

As you can see, in the Blueprint for Success, the Faith pillar covers a lot of ground. There's your faith and spirituality. There's your mindset, thoughts and how you react to things (your EQ), which are influenced by things like what happened in your past and how your brain was designed to work. There's a lot here!

There are also a number of tools you can use to get from wherever you are now in all of this to a better, more successful way of being. I learned many of these tools from my own coach, Nikki Nemerouf. He has helped me so much that I want to give him a shout out here!

Yes, you *can* become more spiritual. You *can* build mental resilience. You *can* learn new ways of responding to situations. You *can* change your thought patterns. You *can* learn to hang out in your wizard brain and only switch to lizard brain mode when there actually is a real danger. You can do this, and when you do, you'll find these things make a huge difference in *all* aspects of your life.

Be open to exploring faith

If all of these ideas are new to you, you may be really struggling with the faith pillar, starting with faith itself. If you're not sure of what to do or how to do it, if you're feeling uncertain or just stuck associating all of this with some bad experiences you had in the past, there's a solution. Expose yourself to people who are happily and successfully leaning into their faith and spirituality.

You don't have to make any commitments. Just dip your toe in the water, and start hanging out with people who are connecting to their higher power. See where that leads you.

The negative forces in the universe don't want you to do anything. They're trying to keep you locked in your current limiting/limited mindset. Tap into the positive forces of the universe – and put yourself in the presence of others who are doing the same – and give faith and spirituality a try.

Understand that there is no "magic pill"

What about all the issues related to mindset, EQ, core beliefs and thoughts? How do you disrupt all this? How do you develop mental toughness and self-discipline? How do you shift your negative or unhelpful thoughts to positive, empowering, helpful thoughts? How do you move away from all these things going on in your brain that are holding you back?

You work on it. And keep working on it and working on it and working on it. I'll be honest. It's really fucking hard. I work on this all the time, because mindset work is a practice game where you have to be hyper-consistent. It's all part of what I said earlier about how if you want to make the Blueprint for Success work you have to be a master of change and habit creation. Because mindset habits can be especially difficult to change, dedication to the process of change – and believing that you *can* change – are musts.

People want a magic pill, a simple answer to how to make more money, lose weight, have better relationships, run their business, etc. When I first started down the personal development journey, I was really just looking for the short cut, too. I went to seminars, joined groups and read books before I finally realized – news flash! – there is no fucking magic pill. There's just commitment, self-discipline and hard work. Consistently doing this work every day, day in and day out for years, is what separates the 1% from everyone else.

Most of the successful people that I know or follow don't come from wealthy families or have impressive degrees from Ivy League colleges. They simply kept working hard and didn't give up. They had grit. If they failed, they learned from the experience and tried again.

Remember what Thomas Edison said about what he went through to invent the electric light bulb? "I have not failed. I've just found 10,000 ways that won't work."

In the rest of this chapter I'll give you tools and practices that are working for me.

Increase your level of grit and self-discipline

One of the first steps towards developing grit and mental toughness is to accept the fact that challenges, issues and breakdowns are going to occur in your life. One of the big reasons you see these events as problems or breakdowns is that you were not expecting them to happen. You were expecting something else – something that would have been more perfectly aligned with your vision, goals and plans.

Stop expecting everything to be perfect!

When unexpected challenges happen, most people's default reaction is to get hyper-locked on the problem. "Why is this happening to me?" they ask. A more empowering response is to shift this question from *"Why* is this happening *to* me?" to *"How* is this happening *for* me?" What is the silver lining? Assume the universe and situation is trying to teach you something valuable, and try to figure out what this is. It's a completely different perspective, and the difference it can make is mind blowing.

Once you learn to shift your initial response, get in the practice of shifting your next response to, "Yeah, this is an issue. Okay, I got it. How do we fix it? What can we learn from it? How can we prevent it from happening again?"

Remember, you become what you think and practice. If you practice seeing every challenge as horrific, every challenge will feel horrific. But when you learn to shift your narrative around challenges and problems, you can create a different, more positive and empowering emotional response to the event. This more positive emotional feeling will change your behavior, which will lead to a more positive and empowering result.

When you're ready to *really* take giant leaps forward in developing your level of grit and self-discipline, I highly recommend you commit to a mental toughness / grit building challenge. For example, I completed a 2-1/2 month program by Andy Frisella called "75 Hard" that, on the surface, appears to be a "fitness and healthy lifestyle" challenge. It didn't take me long, though, to realize that the fitness and healthy lifestyle aspects of this were secondary to the mental toughness it built.

For this challenge, here's what I did every day for 2-1/2 months:

- Worked out twice a day, for at least 45 minutes each time. Regardless of the weather, one of these workouts was outside.

- Eliminated all sugar, sweets and alcohol from my life. This included packaged products that contain sugar. Even most bottled salad dressings were off limits!

- Followed a specific diet that went beyond eliminating sugar and alcohol.

- Drank a gallon of water.

- Read 10 pages of a personal development book.

- Took a full body picture of myself in a bathing suit.

Why was the mental toughness and grit aspect of this harder for me than the diet and exercise? Because the program allowed zero cheating. I committed to following this program *every day for 2-1/2 months,* regardless of what else was happening in my life. If I missed any of these things even once, I had to start again on day one of the 2-1/2 month program.

However you choose to approach this, the more you practice building grit, mental toughness and self-discipline, the stronger you will get emotionally. When this happens, you'll find that issues and challenges that may have upset you or stressed you out five or 10 years ago won't even phase you now. Stuff will happen and your heart won't start racing and you won't fall off the emotional deep end.

Overcome your triggers

Good news! You don't have to leave the relationship / smoke a cigarette / get drunk / quit your job to feel better. In fact, those things probably won't make you feel better in the long term anyway. Instead you can learn to identify and stop your triggered states, so when life happens you can stay in your wizard brain and get access to resolution and positive results.

In fact, overcoming your triggers starts with understanding the concepts of the wizard brain and lizard brain and what's going on with your mindset and emotional states. Then it's a matter of learning new responses.

I'm not going to lie. This takes a lot of practice. It takes time. You're not going to change a lifetime of patterns overnight. It takes a lot of work to unlearn being a highly triggered fight-or-flight person. It takes a lot of work and practice to build new neural pathways in your brain, to change your automatic response to things.

But you can do it. And as a former hothead I'm here to tell you that it's really, really worth it.

Step #1: Recognize that you have a problem

Before you can do something about a problem you must first admit to yourself that you have a problem. You need to become self-aware and identify that there's something going on that's not desirable. You need to be humble and mature with yourself to say that this thing is not serving you and you want to change it.

Chances are everyone around you can clearly see the problem. They all see that you're a hothead, you're overweight, you're broke, you drink too much, you make bad decisions, whatever. Now *you* need to see it clearly, too.

Until you recognize that you have a problem, you won't be motivated to solve it.

For me, I eventually realized that I was an easily-triggered hothead. I saw that I was often behaving in patterns of emotion that were no longer serving me, and I really didn't want to be like this anymore. After all, I cannot be an effective leader, husband, father or friend as a hothead. There's nothing healthy about being a hothead. Who likes being with a hothead? No one.

I realized that I was that person. I was frequently all hopped up. I wasn't solving problems. I was causing problems and making problems worse.

Step #2: *Start to notice how triggers affect you*

Triggers can cause both mild and extreme reactions. You can experience just a slight discomfort, like a mild feeling of anxiety about a situation. You can go into a massive rage. Or you can experience something in between the two.

If you pay close attention, you'll probably start to notice that right before you get into full fight-or-flight mode you have a little sensation. You might feel a little discomfort, anxiety or annoyance. You might feel angry. Your palms might get sweaty. Your mouth might get dry. You might feel a little tension in your gut or your chest.

Any of these can be indicators or signs that you're in a triggered state.

Step #3: *Change your reaction*

Start becoming mindful and aware of these feelings and sensations, because right in that moment between the triggering event and the hormonal surge is your opportunity to take charge and change your reaction.

Assuming you're not actually in danger, that you're simply being triggered, what exactly should you do in that moment? Do nothing. N-o-t-h-i-n-g. Nothing at all. Not fight. Not flight. No action, no reaction, no words you'll regret later, no big decisions or changes, nothing.

Simply step back and be present with your feelings and emotions. Take a deep breath. Or two. Or three. Understand that what's happening now is not really about right now. It's a subconscious reminder of the fear and uncertainty and some type of lack of safety that you had as a child.

Step #4: See the triggering event differently

When an event happens, your brain immediately creates a narrative or story about the event. You immediately see the event a certain way. "Oh, that person is a piece of crap," you tell yourself. "They always do this. They always try to screw me over." That's the type of thing you tell yourself, and it happens so fast that you don't even realize it's happening.

But remember:

Thoughts → Emotions → Behavior → Results

Which means that this story that you tell yourself about the event, this thought, generates an emotion. That emotional state then drives you to have a behavior. That behavior produces a result. And that entire response may have involved a big fight-or-flight response that threw you into lizard brain mode.

But here's the thing. That story you're telling yourself is just a story. It's your interpretation of what happened. And it's your interpretation that triggered the negative feelings. The other person did something that deep down you interpreted as being "not safe." It served as a reminder of something from your past, and this reminder resulted in your emotional state.

Another person might interpret the exact same situation differently. For example, say you're a manager. When an employee is late for work you might get so angry that you're ready to fire him. Another manager might immediately be concerned that something is wrong (their car broke down, their spouse is sick, etc.) and react with empathy instead of anger.

What can you do about this issue? Learn to tell yourself a different type of story about the events that happen. Learn to see things differently. Instead of immediately assuming the worst, seek first to understand. Instead of reacting, try to just breath. Calm your nervous system down. Then respond from a place of calmness instead of anger, in order to change your thoughts about the situation.

Thanks to that confirmation bias thing I was talking about earlier, as humans we think that the stories we tell ourselves are facts. But most of the time when things happen in life our negative assumptions are wrong.

However, you can take command of that narrative and those assumptions and shift into a new, more empowering possibility. This will immediately start to transition you from a lizard brain state of anger, frustration and resentfulness to seeing that maybe there's something going on here that you need to understand.

Let's go back to the example of the tardy employee. Instead of getting triggered you can step back and ask some questions. "I notice you've been late a lot lately," you can say. "Tell me what's happening in your life. What's going on?" Maybe that person is going through some rough stuff. You don't know until you ask.

What about those situations where your default negative assumption about a situation is actually right? Well, being angry with the other person won't solve anything. Being an adult, being a leader, being mature, all mean not letting yourself fly into a rage, because that won't resolve anything. It just keeps you away from your authentic wizard brain self, and pushes everyone else away from you.

When you're always running in a triggered state, you're not leading well. As a result, more problems occur, these problems trigger you and things snowball. Being stressed out, you are in lizard brain mode, so you don't make good decisions and you don't see all the beneficial opportunities.

When you recognize you have a problem, learn to see the triggers and then learn to see these triggering events differently, you start thinking different thoughts. These lead to different, more empowering emotions, which lead to better decisions and actions, which lead to better results.

Your brain is an amazing thing. In some ways it works like a muscle in your body. You can build your muscles by going to the gym and doing reps of weightlifting. You can build new responses by doing reps of healthy practices. The more you practice this, the easier and more automatic it will become.

Identify the core beliefs that are holding you back

As you learned in Chapter 4, you may have deeply ingrained core beliefs that you picked up in childhood. If these are empowering beliefs, great! If not, how can you even know that you *have* a limiting belief? Look backwards at the trends and patterns in your life.

If there's something in your life that keeps going up and down, chances are it's tied to a limiting core belief. Your weight. Your financial situation. Your relationships. Your ability to consistently go to church / act with generosity / have respectful conversations / scale your business / whatever. Wherever you see the pattern that things just keep getting better and worse, better and worse, better and worse, this issue is most likely tied to a limiting core belief.

Something in you strongly believes that you do not deserve success in this area, that you're not enough, that you're not good enough to have it or be it, and your subconscious mind is working hard to ensure you do not get these things.

Here's how that better/worse pattern works. Imagine your subconscious is a thermostat and your limiting belief is the thermostat's "set point." When the temperature in the room goes above a thermostat's set point, the thermostat triggers the air conditioner to kick on in order to bring the temperature back down. Likewise, when you get "too much" of whatever good thing your core belief says you can't have, your subconscious will act like a thermostat and desperately try to bring that "temperature" back down to whatever level your core belief thinks you deserve. You'll start self-sabotaging your success. I know it sounds crazy, but trust me here.

This cycle will keep repeating until you identify that set point – that core belief that's holding you back – and reset it. You need to recognize your faulty core belief for what it is – a thermostat setting that you can change. As a human, you *do* deserve good things. You *are* enough. You *are* good enough to have the things you want in life. You *can* scale your business. You *can* become an amazing leader. You simply need to stop letting that faulty core belief that you internalized during childhood tell you that you aren't. Change the setting on your thermostat.

Visualize and affirm what you want

One way to start changing your core beliefs *and* your thoughts is to use visualization and affirmations.

At least once each day, set aside some time to visualize the things that you want in life. Picture them in great detail. Visualize yourself enjoying these things. Then – here's the super-important part – feel the emotions associated with having these things. *Feel as though you already have it.* Connecting the emotional feelings with the vision is where the magic happens.

For example, say you've been living in apartments your whole life and now you really want to buy a house. But you have a limiting belief that says that owning a home is for "rich people," not you. You don't deserve to own a home. Everyone in your family has always lived in apartments, and that's where you should live, too.

Recognize you've got this core belief and these thoughts, and then use visualization and affirmation to stop the pattern.

Picture the house you want. How big is it? How many bedrooms? How many bathrooms? What's the yard look like? What cool features does it have?

Picture yourself living in the house. See yourself watching the big game on TV while your kids play happily with the neighbor kids in your backyard. Feel a deep sense of gratitude that you can easily afford the mortgage and other costs. See yourself easily paying those bills and see that you still have plenty of money left in your account when you do. Feel the joy of living somewhere that has so much space for your family. Feel that happiness and freedom. Revel in it.

Maybe you're currently running a $5 million business and you want to grow it to $20 million – but that seems so "pie in the sky" that you don't even think it's possible. Instead of letting your fear, uncertainty and limiting beliefs hold you back, shut all that down and replace it with visualizations and affirmations of the amazing business you are building.

For example, visualize yourself being a strong leader. See yourself in the office with a team of successful employees that you're leading, training and coaching. See the amount of money in your bank account going up, up, up. See your company's Chief Financial Officer (because a $20 million company needs a CFO) giving you good news about your company's financial success. See that your business has good structure and organization. Feel how good it feels to be so successful, to be in a position to help others, to be a force of good in this world. Feel happy. Feel confident. Feel wealthy. Feel generous.

As you're visualizing and feeling, affirm your goal in words, too. State the thing that you want in the present tense, *as though you already have it or it is already true*. Not "I wish" or "I want" but "I am" or "I have."

See it, say it, feel it. And do this, consistently, every day. You can even take things one step further and write your affirmations down. That way you can also see the words as you're saying, visualizing and feeling them.

Connect the visualization with the emotion and then further amplify that with words. Through daily repetition of this process you'll begin to reprogram your subconscious mind, so that deep down you will believe that you are already capable of this thing that you want, *and you already have it*. This will enable you to overcome the limiting beliefs that are holding you back so that you will naturally start to move in the direction of turning this vision into a reality. When your subconscious and your body, mind and spirit all believe you're capable or already there, you will start to create it around you.

Repetition is key here. As Napoleon Hill, author of "Think and Grow Rich," one of the greatest self-help books of all time, said, "Any idea, plan or purpose may be placed in the mind through repetition of thought."

Another way to look at this is that you are essentially "tricking" your own brain by changing your thoughts, which will change the "set point" on your thermometer, which will change your results. If you do this consistently, your brain will start to believe these visualizations and affirmations, and your subconscious will start working to make these things happen.

That said, there's something super important that you need to understand about affirmations. *Only* say what you want. *Never* mention anything about what you don't want. This is because the universe and your subconscious mind only hear the thing, not the fact that you don't want it.

Do *not* say, "I'm not poor" or "I don't struggle with money" because saying this is likely to attract more poverty and struggle to your life. Instead, say, "I am a multi-millionaire and my wealth multiplies every day."

It can also be helpful to add a desired emotion to your affirmation.

So instead of "I'm not fat" or "I don't struggle with my weight," you can say, "I love being at my ideal weight" or "I'm grateful that maintaining my ideal weight is so easy and I feel so happy and energetic being in shape."

State what you want and experience the emotion of it, as if you are already there. Don't mention the things that you don't want.

Expose yourself to people who already have what you want

If you want to change your thoughts and beliefs, you have to force yourself out of where you're currently at. One of the best ways to do this is through the power of your "tribe" or network, because the easiest way to change a belief is to start by seeing how this belief is already working for others.

There is a saying that you are the average of the five people you spend the most time with. If this is true, you need to hang out with a network of people who are also on this growth path. This is also part of that Law of Attraction. If you don't believe in a higher power, you'll attract others to you who also don't believe in a higher power. If you believe that you're going great places, you'll attract others who are going there, too.

Here are some things you can do to take advantage of this "power of proximity":

- **Seek out successful people that you already know.** There's always a grandpa, uncle, aunt, neighbor or church member who can be a great mentor.

- **Develop new friendships.** Your current social circle might be holding you back.

- **Follow successful business influencers.** Attend their events, read their books, follow them on social media and join their free groups. Then reach out to let them know that you're interested in learning more about such-and-such from them and ask them if they're open to talking to you about this.

- **Join a leadership group.** A cool thing about today's technology is you can find free groups of people who are leveling up. For example, I have a free Facebook group where people can get exposure to me (you can find this group at www.facebook.com/groups/bluecollarkings).

  There are also many "pay to play" groups, such as business development or personal development groups, which are not free. Depending on who and what you want to expose yourself to regarding business and leadership, one of these groups may be the best option.

For me, when I started putting myself in environments and gatherings where people weren't just successful in terms of their business and money, but were successful in *all* areas of their lives, it showed me what was missing in my own life in terms of faith and spirituality. Seeing is believing, and I saw that their approach to life clearly worked.

While most people default to negative thoughts and negative thinking, I saw that these people – my new tribe – defaulted to the positive. It wasn't "why is this happening to me?" It was "how is this happening for me?" and "what's the lesson I can take from this experience?" Their example helped me change my thoughts and beliefs about what I'm capable of becoming as a husband, father, leader and man.

Get a coach

In addition to all of the things listed above regarding exposing yourself to people who already have what you want, get a coach. This is highly critical.

I have had several coaches over the years who have guided me along my path of changing my mindset, thoughts and core beliefs, and it has been enormously helpful. I have seen firsthand that hands down, by far, having the right coach is the absolute fastest way to grow personally and professionally. I can't stress this enough!

Learn how to meditate

Meditation is all about calming your mind and central nervous system. Meditation can help reduce your stress and anxiety, improve your sleep, increase your ability to concentrate and much more. In addition to all of that, the way I see it is that while *prayer* is *talking* to God, the universe or your higher power, *meditation* is *listening* to God, the universe or your higher power.

Given the many benefits of meditation, it's no wonder pretty much every "how to improve your life" self-help book, seminar, class, etc. recommends meditation. Meanwhile, most people who have actually tried meditation will say something like, "Sure, I tried that, but I couldn't quiet my mind so I decided meditation is not for me."

These people gave up too quickly.

Unless you're lucky and meditation comes naturally to you, it can literally takes months of practice before you start to feel like you're catching on. My own first big breakthrough came after about *four months* of practice! One night I was attempting to meditate but, as usual, my mind kept racing. Then suddenly I was able to look away from those thoughts and briefly experience a really great-feeling state where the thoughts just were not there.

Where you're at today in terms of the activity level of your thoughts and nervous system happened through years and years of practice.

Changing this, even if for just a few minutes, is likely to take a great deal of practice, too.

Today I am usually able to get into a meditative state without a big struggle. How? What's my secret? Keeping in mind that in no way, shape or form do I claim to be like a Buddhist monk who has mastered meditation, here's what's working for me:

- **Get ready to meditate.** Either lay down flat on your back or sit upright in a chair that will support you in sitting up straight.

- **Focus on your breath.** Breath in through your nose and out through your mouth. Some people like to count to four or five while they're breathing in and then count again while they're breathing out. I don't do that. Keep it simple. Just focus on your breath and focus on slowing your breathing down, getting slower and slower with each breath cycle.

- **Don't try to stop your thoughts.** In some meditation practices they'll tell you that the goal is to get your thoughts to stop. "Envision a stop sign in your mind and just tell your thoughts to stop." This has never worked for me. In fact, what I have found is that the more I try to stop my thoughts, the more thoughts come. What you resist in meditation persists or even multiplies.

- **Just be present with your thoughts.** Instead of trying to stop your thoughts, just be present with the thoughts you're having. Let them flow and let them pass. To me the art of the game is not stopping the thoughts – it's acknowledging the thoughts and then essentially looking away and ignoring them.

  Here's a way to see this. Imagine you're in Las Vegas at a *huge* slot machine. When you pull the handle, a whole bunch of wheels start spinning. Your thoughts are like those spinning wheels. You might have seemingly thousands of thoughts spinning, spinning, spinning in your mind.

When those wheels become present in your mind, just let them run. Then think, "Thank you for spinning, but I'm not interested in looking at you now." In your mind, look away from all those spinning wheels and look at a mental image of darkness or stars or the universe instead.

- **Refocus your mind away from your thoughts.** As more thoughts come, be grateful or present with these thoughts. Don't resist. Then say, "Thank you, I'm not going to look at you anymore," and refocus your mind on that image of darkness, stars or the universe.

Finally, recognize that meditation is helpful even if it's not perfect. Just taking some time each day (or, ideally, multiple times each day) to slow your breathing down can have a calming and relaxing effect, even if you're not yet succeeding in turning your mind away from the enticement of all those "spinning wheels" that are your thoughts.

Establish a beneficial daily routine

Remember, there is no "magic pill." Getting and keeping your mindset and thoughts where you want them to be is not a "one and done" type of thing. It's something you need to work on and be aware of every day.

These practices are also not things that are likely to feel natural to you. Which means that you can't just try, say, meditation, for a week or two, think "This doesn't work," and then give up. You have to keep at it.

Here's what works for me. Try it and see if it works for you!

15-minute morning routine

- **Pray or meditate:** As soon as you wake up in the morning, say a short prayer. If prayer isn't your thing, try doing a brief meditation instead.

- **Write in a gratitude journal:** After that, write down five things that you are grateful for. I have a special "Gratitude Journal" that I use for this, but you can also just use a spiral notebook. Write the date and "I am grateful for" at the top of the page, and then write down five things as bullet points.

The important thing here is that when you are writing down the thing that you are grateful for you also need to remember the *feeling* you had when you were experiencing that thing. So, for example, if you say you are grateful for your spouse, include at least one reason *why* you are grateful for your spouse. For example, "I am grateful for Heather because she makes me feel loved and appreciated." Then take a moment to experience that *feeling* of being loved and appreciated. If you write, "I am grateful that we landed that big account yesterday," think about how good you felt when you got the news.

- **Connect with nature:** I think it's important to experience a little piece of Mother Nature each morning. Step outside and take some deep breaths. Look up into the sun and get some sunlight in your eyes. If that's not possible or practical, open a window and get a breath of fresh air, or at least open the blinds and look outside. All it takes is a minute to get that connection.

5- to 10-minute afternoon routine

Try to establish a consistent time in the afternoon when you take a break from work or life or whatever you are doing in order to pray or meditate.

5- to 10-minute bedtime routine

Before you go to bed, do another prayer or meditation. I like to tell God what I'm grateful for; ask for knowledge, wisdom and leadership; and ask for help and insight regarding anything that is challenging me.

Then do your visualizations and affirmations as outlined earlier in this chapter. Visualize and affirm the things you are striving to create in your life, always feeling the associated emotions as though you already have these things.

Remember, it takes time to establish a new habit. After following these practices (or something similar) every day for three months, it will become routine. If you have been struggling with negativity, you'll be amazed at how much your mindset will change.

CHAPTER 7:

UNDERSTANDING THE FAMILY PILLAR

The Family pillar of the Blueprint for Success is all about relationships – from your relationships with your family and friends to your relationships with the people that you work with.

As I mentioned earlier, there's a saying that you are the average of the five people that you spend the most time with. Who are these people? What type of relationships do you have with each of them? Are these relationships serving you well? If not, did you know that you can take action to change this?

Start influencing the quality of your relationships

When I look around, I realize that most people are operating in what I would call an almost trance-like state. They're like robots. They just show up to life and do the same things over and over again, without giving it much thought. Then they just accept or react to whatever happens. It doesn't occur to them that *they can influence what happens.*

I used to be this way. I just showed up. When I wasn't happy with how my relationships were going, I figured this was just the way things were.

When I came to understand that I could influence these things, it was a big breakthrough for me. It might be a breakthrough for you, too!

The reality is you can actually have a lot of command and control over the quality of your relationships. You are the captain of that ship, and you have the wheel of that ship in your hands. If your relationships do not currently feel like part of the life of abundance and fulfillment that you want to create, you can steer the ship in a different direction to change your relationships for the better.

Begin with an evaluation

Before you can steer the ship you need to have a feel for where you are and where you want to go. This starts with awareness, so the first step is to evaluate where things currently stand. Evaluating your relationships means asking some important questions that you may not have thought about before.

For example, what is the quality of your interactions with your friends? Are you building close and trusting relationships with your spouse and kids? What types of things do you talk about? What types of things do you not talk about? How do you and these people react to each other when there are disagreements or different points of view? How much thought and effort are you currently putting into being a good spouse, parent, friend, neighbor, boss or co-worker?

Who is your best friend – and why? What "best" things are happening with this friend? Are you growing together and doing good things together? Are your families intertwined? What are you doing when you get together? Are you just showing up, drinking beer and complaining about stuff? Or are you showing up to do things and talk about things that are empowering and that help each other become better humans?

Have you ever even thought about the content of the conversations you and your friends and family typically have? I never used to, but now I've become super-aware of it. And super annoyed when people just want to rehash dramas, complain or have a pity party. You know how it goes. "I can't believe my wife said such-and-such" or "My boss is such a jerk, showing up for work is just misery" or "Did you see the latest news? Man, our country sucks right now!"

As if all these complaints aren't bad enough, because the complainers just seem to attract each other, they end up in a big group of victims. Then the whole event becomes one big sob story about how horrible life is.

Is this really what you want? I sure don't. I don't want to hang out with people who do nothing but whine and complain. I recommend that you don't do so, either.

Instead, surround yourself with people who want to have empowering conversations and talk about positive things, especially regarding creativity, spirituality or events. For example, reminisce about great memories. Hear about the cool fishing trip they just took or the award their kid won. Ask them to tell you about something they're working on or planning, or some of the interesting things they've been thinking about. If they start whining and complaining, shut it down and try to steer the conversation a different way instead.

When I first started evaluating my own relationships, I realized that some of my friendships were not as great as they could be. We were doing fun activities, like camping or off roading, but our conversations were not empowering. Things weren't ideal between me and my wife, Heather, either. Sure, I loved her deeply – but what was I doing to show it? Instead of working to grow our love and our relationship, I had just been showing up and being reactive. I realized it was up to me to change.

Be more intentional and less expectational

What I've seen is that we all tend to be very expectational in relationships. We *expect* a lot of other people. Then we get locked in on what they are *not* doing, meaning all the different ways they are not meeting our expectations.

But here's the thing. When you expect a lot of other people, you're setting yourself up to be unhappy. Expectations are like premeditated resentments and disappointments. You set expectations and then you feel disappointed and resentful when the other person doesn't live up to those expectations. But maybe the problem isn't the other person. Maybe the problem is you, and the "measuring stick" that you're using to "measure" them.

There are over eight billion people on the planet, and no two people see the world exactly the same way. So why is it that we tend to see other people not as *they* are, but as *we* are? We expect them to think and act and speak and make decisions just like we do. Then when they don't measure up to that expectation, we're disappointed and resentful.

In relationships it's much better to be more intentional and less expectational. When you're expectational it's hard to see the gifts that others bring and to appreciate their differences. But when you focus on your *intention* to create really good relationships, it's easier to focus on the positive.

Learn to love yourself

As you're working on being more intentional and less expectational, the best place to start is your relationship with yourself.

Let go of your unhelpful thoughts from the past, such as, "I'm not enough," "I don't deserve good things," "I always screw things up," etc. Learn to love and appreciate yourself instead.

The cleaner you get with yourself in terms of how you live your life, starting with the absolute values of truth and integrity that form the foundation of the Blueprint for Success, the more the way you see the world will evolve and change for the better. It gets easier to appreciate your own strengths, forgive your own failings and commit to improvement.

Things will never be perfect in any of your relationships – including your relationship with yourself – so add that to the list of expectations to ditch. Instead of perfection, shoot for progress, growth and development.

Be the change that you want

One of the things I've learned is that as long as you're waiting for others to change, you're actually pushing the positive outcomes away. You need to be the change that you want. Remember, you are becoming a master of change and a master of creating new habits. This is key to making the Blueprint for Success work for you.

Being the change you want is especially critical in your relationship with your spouse. If your spouse wants to jointly commit to working together to grow your relationship, like my wife did, great! If you're not even at the point where you feel comfortable having that conversation, start acting as though they're already on board. Figure out what things make them feel most loved and cherished, the things that matter the most to them in your relationship, and do these things. Every day. With love in your heart, and without any expectations regarding how they'll respond. Create a new habit of consistently doing the things that matter most to your spouse.

If you've been in a relationship in which you've just been showing up and taking, taking, taking without ever giving back in ways that actually matter to the other person, how do you think they're currently feeling? Unloved? Resentful? Exhausted? Empty? Tired of trying to steer the ship towards "happiness and fulfillment island" while you keep throwing down the anchor elsewhere?

Especially if you've just been showing up by default, it's on you to be the change you want. Start taking proactive beneficial action to grow your relationships.

This is not about expecting someone else to do something for you and complaining when they don't. It's about being intentional in your own words and actions. It's about helping them, showing and demonstrating your feelings for them and appreciating what they bring to the table in your relationship. It's about doing the things that are in your power to move the relationship in a better direction.

As part of this, you need to be sure to leave room in the relationship for the other person to be different than you, and to do things that you may not totally agree with. Learn to have productive conversations around your differences. Leave space for the other person, and leave space for these conversations!

Understand that you don't have to be best buddies with your co-workers

Many people want to be friends with the people they work with. After all, you spend a lot of time with your co-workers. Shouldn't you all be pals? Not necessarily.

Remember, your primary mission at work is not to have fun. You are there to ethically get work done, make money and produce a result for everyone's financial gain. Your goal should be to have professional, respectful and cordial relationships with your co-workers, and strive to do your part to work well with them. You want to have positive, empowering relationships. But these can be "professional relationships," not "personal friendships."

If you are *not* in a leadership position and you happen to become personal friends with a co-worker, that's okay – as long as you do not let this relationship interfere with your work or have a negative impact on your team's overall dynamics.

If you *are* in a leadership position, you may need to avoid developing personal friendships with those who are below you on the organizational chart. These relationships can impact your ability to lead, and are a slippery slope that can quickly lead to a lose-lose situation. Others on your team are bound to assume you are favoring your friend, even if you're bending over backwards to hold everyone to the same standards. Meanwhile, your friend may not respect you as their "boss," and may not be receptive when you attempt to coach them, hold them accountable when they miss the mark, etc. You may even avoid holding your friend accountable, for fear that it will impact your friendship.

Am I saying that you can never be close friends with a coworker or someone that you lead? No. But I want you to be aware that if you are, you need to have very professional and respectful boundaries. If you are a leader you must make it clear – and the friend who is an employee must understand – that when it comes to work, you do things 100% by the book. Absolutely no favoritism or nepotism.

Recognize that you may need new friends

I mentioned this before in reference to changing your thoughts and beliefs, and understanding the power of your "tribe." I'll mention it again here in the context of having empowering and fulfilling relationships. Through all of this work you may find that some of your friends and relationships aren't serving you anymore. It's not necessarily that you don't care about these people. It's that you may now choose to expose yourself to different activities in life, and to hang out with people who want to talk about more uplifting things that are more beneficial for both of you. You may need to develop new friendships.

Please note that I am *not* saying you should divorce your spouse if they're not (yet) on the "continuous growth" bandwagon. You made a lifetime vow to this person and it's on you to honor this commitment, be the change that you want to see and work to make things better.

But you might find that there are others in your life who really shouldn't be there anymore.

Key Points for Chapter 7

- You *can* influence the quality of your relationships.

- Start by learning to love yourself. Appreciate your strengths, forgive your failings and commit to improvement.

- Be the change you want. Don't wait for others to make things happen.

- Treat your co-workers with professionalism and respect. You don't have to be best buddies.

- Recognize that you may need new friends.

Chapter 7 Exercise

Evaluate where things currently stand in the major relationships in your life. Be honest with yourself. Are you having empowering interactions? What role are you playing in this? Are you just showing up, or are you putting thought and effort into the relationship? If things are not ideal, are you ready to take action to change this?

CHAPTER 8:

IMPLEMENTING THE PRINCIPLES OF THE FAMILY PILLAR

Your life is full of relationships! You have relationships with your extended family. If you're married and/or a parent, you have relationships with your spouse and kids. You have relationships with your friends, neighbors, co-workers, boss or employees, and more. How you approach and manage all of these relationships will have a huge impact on your happiness. How you deal with your work-related relationships can also have a big impact on your career or business success.

The good news is, as discussed in Chapter 7, you *can* have a lot of command and control over the quality of your relationships, and if things are not the way you want them to be, you *can* take action to improve them. You are becoming a master of change. You *can* do it! This chapter provides some tools to implement and new habits and behaviors to create that can help you increase and then maintain the quality of your relationships.

Create core values for your family

In Chapter 2 you learned that core values are a key part of the Foundation of the Blueprint for Success, and you learned the process for defining your own core values. If you are married or in a long-term committed relationship, I strongly recommend that the two of you work together to create a set of core values for your household – values that you both agree your family will live by. If you are single, you'll need to do this on your own.

Once you have this defined, memorize it and talk and think about it regularly.

For example, my wife and I went through the process and defined our core values for our life together. We came up with Honor, Excellence, Leadership, Adventure and Grit.

A nice thing about this is that when we notice that the other person is straying from these values, it takes away the "you vs. me" dynamic. We made an agreement to strive to live by these values. Without getting all worked up, one of us can say, "I don't think you're living in alignment with the Excellence value today" without starting a fight. Instead of feeling judged, we're both judging ourselves against the same standard.

Date your spouse

When you first start dating someone, hormones are high, emotions are high and because of these things you tend to do extra things for that person that you wouldn't normally do in a long-term relationship. Then you wonder why the "magic" in the relationship just seems to be missing. However, these things you used to do and the strong chemistry between you don't have to go away. We let them go away because we get comfortable and complacent. But we can be intentional about bringing them back.

My wife Heather and I proactively work to do these things. I date my wife. I still give her little love notes. I send little texts throughout the day. Because I know that Heather feels loved when I do things for her to ease her burden, I do things that will ease her burden, such as grocery shopping.

Every Wednesday night the two of us are on Date Night. This is mandatory for us. It's not optional. It's not something that gets done just when it's convenient, or behind kids, work, laundry, etc. Every Wednesday night is Date Night. It is absolute. It has to be done.

What do we do on Date Night? Something fun! And not always the same thing. We change it up and keep it fresh.

Why do we do these things? Because going out and having fun, just the two of us, helps keep the magic, passion and energy alive!

If you are married or in a long-term relationship that's past that "first love" phase, you should date your partner, too.

Have quality time with your spouse every day

A weekly Date Night alone is not enough to keep the spark and magic alive in your marriage. Your relationship requires time and attention every day. So in addition to Date Night, set aside at least some time each day for the two of you. No news, no social media, no email, no work, no work talk. Just time to enjoy each other's company and connect.

As part of this quality time the two of you should also do a daily check-in with each other.

If you're working to grow a relationship, the two of you must agree to allow feedback, because nothing can improve without some data points. There has to be space and trust where constructive, loving feedback is permitted.

This is where the core values that we discussed in Chapter 2 come in. Your core values are an extremely useful tool that provides some guiding principles for your relationship, allowing you to identify what is working and what is not working without defensiveness. You've already agreed on the values. Are you living up to them or not?

What I recommend is that you use your core values as a framework for a daily check-in. Have a daily micro-conversation about what is working and what is not. It's very soft. And it requires both of you to show up with a spirit of openness and humility to hear the other person, to listen without debating things that you don't agree with.

That said, it's important that you don't just focus on the negative. Where people often miss the mark, especially in regard to their spouse, is that they get really good at identifying what their spouse is not doing, or what their spouse is doing that is pissing them off. All of the positive stuff gets overlooked.

To ensure you don't just focus on the negative, use the "sandwich method" of feedback. Start with something positive (that's the bottom slice of bread in the sandwich). Then give an idea for improvement (that's the meat in the middle of the sandwich). Then end with another positive (that's the top slice of bread in the sandwich).

If the two of you are having a hard time thinking of what to say, ask each other questions, such as: What do you want me to keep doing? What would you like more of in our relationship that I am doing for you? What is not working? What would you like less of? What else is making you happy?

A daily check-in like this will keep you on track, while also keeping you from getting hyper locked in on the negative and losing sight of all the good that is happening.

Plus, if you get into the rhythm of doing this on the micro then you can usually avoid a lot of macro, bigger problems. If you're having daily conversations and constantly optimizing, little issues won't have a chance to grow into big issues.

Instill your core values in your kids

Putting your family's core values into action requires constant repetition and reinforcement. Repeat them often, so they become ingrained in your children's minds.

- **When your kids are young, repeat your core values as a mantra.** For example, when her kids were growing up, one of my friends constantly repeated the mantra, "In our home we treat each other with love, respect, understanding and kindness." This mantra was a reflection of her family's core values.

- **Have a time each day when you always talk about core values.** This can be on the way to or from school, at the dinner table, etc. During this discussion you state the core values together and then have each person (including you!) share an example of how they recently lived these core values.

  "Alright, cool," you can say, "now can you give me an example of how you were living one of these core values this week?" If they need more prompting, you can say something like, "Tell me something you did to be a good leader in school."

- **Look for opportunities to praise your kids' positive behavior in terms of your core values.** "I love the way you honored your brother by including him in the fun when your friend came over today." "I noticed that you really put a lot of effort into making your school project excellent." And so forth.

- **Use the core values when you need to discipline your children.**
One of the huge powers of having a set of core values for your family is that it creates a framework for discipline and feedback that is far less confrontational and emotionally triggering than other approaches. This is because instead of telling your child, "Don't do that" or "That pisses me off," you're identifying an undesirable behavior using the core values as the guidelines.

First, make sure that you are not triggered yourself. If you're in your lizard brain you'll trigger them to get into lizard brain, too, and then by default they'll resist whatever you are trying to teach them. Once you are certain you are in wizard brain, simply ask, "Do you think what you're doing right now is in line with our core values?" If they say yes, say, "Let's discuss it" and ask them to explain their thoughts. Then guide them towards understanding why their behavior was undesirable.

If they say no, their behavior was not in alignment with your family's core values, say, "Thank you!" Ask them to explain why they were doing that, and then ask them, "Can you make a commitment to me not to do that anymore?" This way they give you their word that they will do their best to change their behavior. Once they give this commitment thank them, and have them make any necessary amends.

Note that very young children are not likely to be able to make the connections between their behavior and your family's core values on their own. You need to help them. "How do you think your brother felt when you took away his toy? Was that loving? Was that respectful? Was that kind? Next time let's try to remember that in our home we treat each other with love, respect, understanding and kindness."

Remember, disciplining your children is all about helping them learn responsible behavior and self-control. It is guidance and coaching. "Discipline" does *not* mean "punishment."

Spend quality time with your kids

A lot of parents get caught up in the idea that they must be with their kids all the time. If they can't be there every day, helping them with their homework, taking them to activities, cheering them on at every sports practice and so forth, they think they're bad parents. They measure their worth as parents in terms of linear time spent with their kids.

But we as humans don't measure it that way. If you look back on your own childhood you'll realize that we don't have the brain capacity to remember quantifiable units of time spent together. What we remember are the experiences and the emotions.

What this means is that if someone has the luxury of being a full-time parent (as well as the desire to do this), great. There's absolutely nothing wrong with that. But if you don't, this does not mean that you are a bad parent. Either way, you need to focus on the experiences and the emotions that you are creating when you *are* with your children. In the long term, these are the things that they will remember. They'll remember the experiences – both good and bad – and the emotional states they associate with these experiences.

Remember when we were talking about mindset and EQ, and how things that happen in your life can trigger an emotional response based on traumatic events from your childhood? What this means for you as a parent is that if the way that you interact with your children causes them a lot of stress and trauma, if your behavior fails to make them feel loved and safe, then you are not just failing them now. You are also setting them up for years of challenges.

So what do I recommend you do? Here are some ideas:

- **Have a weekly "family fun day"** – At least once a week get out and go on an outing together as a family. This doesn't have to be an expensive trip to an amusement park. If you're on a tight budget, research low-cost things to do in your area. You can go to the beach, take a hike, go for a bike ride, fly kites, head to the local children's museum or do whatever your kids would enjoy. Be spontaneous. Make it fun!

- **Create an environment of trust** – You have to set up a trust zone with your kids in which you both can communicate what's working and what's not. You need to help them understand that it's okay to tell you the truth, even if they did something wrong. You need to demonstrate, over and over, that if they do tell you the truth, they can trust you not to explode in anger. Because if they think you may go crazy with angry, negative emotions, they won't feel safe sharing anything with you at all.

Here's what I recently started doing to create this environment of trust with my own kids, who at the time I'm writing this are 10 and 11 years old. I've set up a routine. Every night I tuck my kids into bed. I give them love and affection. I make them feel safe. We pray together. We talk. I ask them what they're happy about and what they're grateful for. I praise their positive behavior, telling them what I'm proud of.

If they missed the mark in some way that day, I make it a point to discuss it long before bedtime, because I don't want that to be the last thing on their mind when they nod off to sleep.

But I don't just make this feedback about them. I give them space to provide feedback to me, too. I ask them to tell me what I do that makes them feel uncertain, sad or scared. I ask them what I do that makes them feel happy and loved. I also ask if there's anything bothering them (whether or not it's about me) that they want to talk about. While I know that this process will take time, I am working hard to create a safe space in which they can share.

Create great experiences

In all of your personal relationships, be in the business of creating positive, fun, empowering experiences. Don't wait for other people to set something up. Be the one who takes action.

Make a commitment to go out of your way to do things for others. Surprise your kids with a trip to the park or the beach or whatever they would enjoy. Surprise your spouse with a fun date night. Leave a playful note on your spouse's car like you used to do when you were dating. Tap into that energy to keep the excitement alive in your relationships. Be consistently spontaneous!

Reach out to your friends and set up a barbecue, weekend getaway, spa day, movie night or whatever. Don't let the bonds of friendship start to fizzle out because you're both getting stuck in "why should I be the one to reach out – he never seems to reach out to me" mode. Who cares if it's not "your turn" to initiate contact? Do it anyway. Be the one that your friends admire because you're so incredibly good at staying in touch and coming up with fun reasons to get together.

Think about how you can create "Wow!" experiences for others. Try something new. Get outside of your box and comfort zone and break the mold of whatever you and the people in your life have been doing. Or, if there's something you all really enjoy, be the one who makes sure that you regularly get out there and do it.

How can you come up with ideas for these amazing experiences? There's a seemingly never-ending supply of ideas online. Look at social media to see what your friends are doing. Google "things to do this month in my city" and see what comes up. Google "fun things to do with kids on a budget" or "great ideas for date nights" or "best things to do in my area." It's also helpful to get on the email distribution lists for the entertainment venues you like, such as the local comedy club or music venue, so that you always know what's coming up.

You can have a lot of fun and make people feel good by being in the business of creating great experiences, and living that way all the time. It's not that hard. Figure it out and go have fun. Do it!

CHAPTER 9:

UNDERSTANDING THE FITNESS PILLAR

The Fitness pillar is about everything related to how you treat and/or take care of your body. This includes exercise, diet, sleep and more. Statistically speaking, you have a much higher likelihood of living a long, healthy life if you have a healthy diet and lifestyle. But as so many New Year's resolutions reflect, this area is a real challenge for most of us.

I am certainly no exception here. I do not claim to be a fitness, health or nutrition expert. In fact, of all the pillars of the Blueprint for Success framework, the area of health, fitness and nutrition has always been my weak point, my "kryptonite."

This pillar of the Blueprint might be your "kryptonite," too. If it is, remember what I said in Chapter 1. Instead of running from your weak pillar, you need to embrace the fact that this is simply harder for you, and lean into mastering it anyway. Otherwise your weak pillar will act as a roadblock for you, and this roadblock will affect *all* aspects of your life and all the other pillars, not just that one.

I was really surprised to see the difference that leaning into the Fitness pillar made in my own life. Once I cut out alcohol and obsessive eating, lost weight and got my health in order, I found that I had greater mental clarity, which is very important for a leader. I noticed a positive impact on my EQ, which helped my relationships. Plus, I slept better, had more energy and felt better overall. It was a *huge* change for the better!

Plus, the positivity and momentum I experienced from conquering my weak pillar transferred to my other pillars and gave me rocket fuel there.

What it means to have a healthy lifestyle

There's a lot more to having a healthy diet and lifestyle than you might realize. The Fitness pillar includes *everything* related to how you treat or take care of your body. This includes:

- Exercise

- Diet

- Hydration

- Sleep

- TV and screen time

- "Poisons"

- Mindset

The benefits of having a healthy lifestyle

There are so many benefits of having a healthy diet and lifestyle, including exercising regularly, that once you start to make progress in this area you'll wonder what took you so long to get with the program. By embracing the Fitness pillar you can:

- **Reduce your risk of some serious diseases**, including heart disease (the number one cause of death for Americans), type 2 diabetes, stroke and some cancers.

- **Boost your immune system**, so you'll be less likely to catch every cold and flu that breezes by.

- **Have more energy throughout the day**, because you are eating the right foods to fuel your system without causing big blood sugar spikes and drops.

- **Improve your hormonal balance**, which can help you feel better all around. Your hormones affect your energy, focus, sleep, level of stress and anxiety, mood and more.

- **Achieve and maintain a healthy weight.** It is estimated that 75% of men and 67% of women are either overweight or obese.

- **Strengthen your bones and muscles**, which is especially important as you age.

- **Improve your physique**, which in many ways is an outer projection of your inner world. If you can't manage your own "body temple," you're really going to struggle with achieving a holistic balance in your life.

- **Help your digestive system function well**, which is always a good thing.

- **And more.**

Why exercise

When I first started exercising I thought that the only real benefit of exercise was to build muscle and self-discipline. It turns out that these things are just the tip of the iceberg. Getting regular exercise also has emotional, psychological and overall health benefits, as well.

For example, cardio exercise releases endorphins. Endorphins are the "feel good" hormones, so this helps you have a more positive outlook on life. Ever hear of "runner's high?" You don't have to run a marathon to experience that endorphin rush! Exercise can also improve your memory and brain function, heart health, immune system, confidence, sleep and more.

Having a physical job isn't enough

I talk to a lot of guys who say, "Why the hell do I need to go to the gym? I'm an HVAC technician (or a plumber or an auto mechanic or whatever). I'm 'exercising' all day, just to do my job."

If you have a physical job, deliberate exercise can help you to do that job better *and* reduce the chance of injuries. The key here is to develop an exercise program that complements the exercise you get at work and helps you build the endurance to do those things at work.

If your job involves lifting, lifting weights at the gym can help ensure you have the muscles to safely do that lifting on the job. You want back strength, shoulder strength, leg strength, etc., so that your biceps are not doing all the work.

If your job involves mostly staying in one place all day, you also need to do cardio exercise, such as jogging or walking, to keep your heart healthy. The physical activity you do at work probably isn't intense enough to provide big cardiovascular benefits.

If your job involves a lot of repetitive motion, having a strong and healthy body can help you to do these repetitive motions without getting injured.

In addition to all of these physical things, a big reason to commit to a regular exercise program is that doing so develops self-confidence, mental toughness and grit – and these things will then help you with all other aspects of the Blueprint for Success, too.

Most processed foods are not good for you

If you've been putting a bunch of crap into your body, think hard about the old saying, "You are what you eat." Think about what these foods are doing to your health. Do you want your body and your health to be crappy?

Some foods are obviously crap, like junk foods. After all, we even call them "junk." Others are things that you might think are reasonably healthy, but aren't. Most processed foods probably fall into the "not healthy" category, because of all the sugars and artificial preservatives that they usually contain.

Like I said, I'm not a dietitian or nutritionist or any other type of nutrition expert. But I have been educating myself about this, and one of the things I've learned is that if you look closely at the ingredients and "Nutrition Facts" of the foods that you eat, it can be a real eye opener.

For example, you might grab a package of Wheat Thins® crackers off the shelf at the grocery store and think, "It's *Wheat* Thins®. How bad can that be? It's wheat, right?" Well if you turn that box over and look at the ingredients, you'll see that out of the 10 ingredients in the list, three are sugar. Of course, seemingly just to trick you into thinking these crackers aren't that unhealthy, two of these types of sugar aren't listed as "sugar." They're listed as "malt syrup (from corn and barley)" and "refiner's syrup."

Here's a label-reading tip: In packaged foods, "syrup" is another word for "sugar."

Next look at the Nutrition Facts panel, where it says that for every 16 of those little crackers you eat (and who can eat less than 16?) you'll be eating 4 grams of added sugars. Which doesn't sound like that much, but 4 grams is a teaspoon of sugar. So every time you eat a couple handfuls of Wheat Thins® you're eating an entire spoonful of sugar. Who knew?

The point is, don't just assume something is healthy or "not that bad." Read the ingredient statement and Nutrition Facts and see what you're really putting into your body.

Added sugars are not good for you

Why am I making such a fuss about sugar – specifically added sugar? Because it's not good for you. "Added sugars" are the sugars that product manufacturers add in to make their products taste sweet. This is different than "natural sugars," which are the sugars naturally found in foods like fruits, vegetables and dairy products.

According to the American Heart Association, consuming too much added sugar can put you at higher risk for cardiovascular disease, cognitive problems such as dementia and Alzheimer's disease, colon cancer, pancreatic cancer, diabetes, high blood pressure, kidney disease, liver disease, obesity and more. Is dealing with any of these things part of your vision for the abundantly fulfilled lifestyle you want to enjoy?

Many preservatives are not good for you

The ingredients list of those Wheat Thins® also says, "BHT added to packaging material to preserve freshness." BHT is a preservative that prevents oils in food from oxidizing and becoming rancid.

If you Google it, you'll see that although the U.S. government says BHT is "generally recognized as safe when used in an approved manner," other countries have banned it. Why? Because in those other countries, people believe the research that says that BHT can cause cancer as well as liver, thyroid and kidney problems.

BHT can even impact testosterone levels. Let's be honest, gentlemen. Who wants to do anything that might lower your testosterone levels? No man I've ever met wants to do anything to lower testosterone. And women, this can be bad for you, too!

I haven't done any research on any of the other preservatives that are commonly found in foods, but chances are their safety is controversial, too.

While I personally doubt a tiny little bit of BHT or other common preservative will cause any of these problems, the issue is that if you eat lots of things that contain this ingredient, your total exposure can add up.

GMOs may not be good for you

"GMOs" are "genetically modified organisms," in this case plants such as corn and soy that scientists have changed at the genetic DNA level. They do this genetic engineering to accomplish some goal such as making the plant grow differently or to increase crop yield by making the plant itself resistant to pests and disease. A lot of crops have been changed so that they're resistant to herbicides. So now farmers can spray the heck out of their fields with something to kill the weeds and they won't also kill the crops.

GMOs were first introduced into our food supply in the early 1990s. Today nearly all the soybeans, corn, canola, sugar beets and cotton grown in the U.S. are GMO crops. Since most processed foods contain ingredients that come from soy, corn, canola and/or sugar beets, most processed foods contain GMOs.

So what's the big deal here? Are GMOs okay to eat or not?

Well, it depends on who you ask, because it's a *very* controversial issue. According to the U.S. government, GMOs are fine. According to a lot of other people, they may not be. Interestingly, there's a long list of countries that have banned the cultivation of GMO crops, yet still allow GMO foods to be imported.

As far as I can tell from my research, they didn't do long-term tests *in humans* to figure out if this stuff is safe or not before it took over the food supply. I've seen some studies regarding how GMOs affect animals that found that GMOs *might* have toxic effects on an animal's liver, pancreas and other organs, as well as its reproductive systems. But these studies were not conclusive.

Like I said, it's controversial. You'll have to decide for yourself if you're concerned.

If it sounds like a chemical it probably isn't good for you

Here's another little "how to read an ingredient list" trick I learned. If there's something in the list that looks like a scientific term, sounds like it's in some other language or is an abbreviation, just assume it's bad for you! For example, "dextrose," "fructose" and "sucrose" are all sugars. "Butylated hydroxytoluene" and "sodium benzoate" are preservatives. To eat a healthier diet, stick with easily recognizable ingredients.

Your entire body needs proper hydration

For a long time I didn't focus on water and hydration, because I didn't understand how important it is. As it turns out, our bodies are made up of about 55 to 60% water (55% for adult women and 60% for adult men). More than half your body is water! Most of that water is located in your cells, where it makes up about 70% or more of your total cell mass.

Your organs, tissues, bones, etc. are made of cells, and these cells contain a lot of water. Your blood is about 81% water. Your liver is about 71% water. Not surprisingly, given their hardness, your bones are not so full of water – only about 22%. And here's the one that really surprised me: Your brain is about 75% water.

Why should you care? Because this helps you understand why, if you are not consuming enough water to meet your body's needs for hydration, your body, including your brain, is not going to function well. Hydration affects your body, mindset, emotions, intellect and nearly everything else.

But "hydration" does not mean "any liquid will do."

I used to drink a lot of sodas and energy drinks. I didn't realize how bad these are for you, especially the energy drinks. Besides all the negatives of the sugar and chemicals, that super-high jolt of caffeine that you get from energy drinks can actually *dehydrate* your body instead of hydrating it.

Alcohol is dehydrating, too. What about coffee? It depends on how much you drink. In moderation, coffee is hydrating. Drink too much and it can be dehydrating.

Sleep is important for your overall health

According to our government (specifically, a survey completed by the Centers for Disease Control and Prevention), more than a third of Americans are sleep-deprived. Many who took the survey even admitted to having fallen asleep at the wheel in the prior month. Wow!

When I was younger – and I'm guessing the same holds true for most of us – I felt like I could get by and sustain with less sleep. But maybe I was just fooling myself. Maybe I was so used to being sleep-deprived that I didn't even notice what it was doing to me.

Sleep impacts your brain performance, mood and overall health. Sleep can help you think more clearly, feel less stressed, stay at a healthy weight and boost your immune system. But if you regularly do not get enough sleep, this increases your risk for a whole bunch of diseases and conditions, including stroke, heart disease, dementia and obesity.

While you are sleeping, your body and brain are actually quite busy repairing cells, getting rid of toxins, releasing hormones and more. When you don't get enough sleep, these things do not happen the way they should. Even just regularly getting one hour less sleep than what your body needs can cause problems that go beyond the obvious issues that you may notice with your focus, emotional control and energy levels.

Most adults need seven or more hours of sleep each night. Personally, I've found that seven hours is the sweet spot for me.

Your screen time might be negatively affecting you

Your TV, computer, cell phone and tablet all emit what's known as "blue light." Blue light wakes us and stimulates us, and can also stimulate your internal biological clock and disrupt your natural sleep cycles. So blue light can be a problem.

Personally, I have a very active mind and high energy, and my brain seems to be highly respondent to blue light. So I'm actively working on just not being on my phone so much.

Beyond the blue light issue, you also need to be concerned with addiction. While I see that our smart phones can be great tools with empowering and positive benefits, they can also turn into an addiction as well. Social media, for example, is designed to be addictive. Social media is designed so that every time you get a "like" or comment on your posts, or even just see posts that you agree with, your brain will release dopamine. Because dopamine is the "feel good" hormone, those dopamine hits are like drugs, and you naturally want more, more, more.

In our society it seems like the expectation is that we all have to be available all the time. I've worked hard to shift my mindset around the idea that this isn't true. I do *not* need to always be immediately available to everyone on the planet who has my email, phone number or social media handles.

I used to be the guy who wanted to answer every email, text and social media message *right away*. I didn't want to disappoint someone or leave someone hanging. I was constantly checking my messages to see if anything came in, starting from the moment I woke up in the morning until the moment I went to bed at night.

Now I'm relentless about not looking at my phone at all (other than swiping left to turn my alarm off) until the entire morning routine that I talked about in Chapter 6 is done. When I start my day by taking care of myself first, I feel a lot better and my day goes a lot smoother. Then I aim to turn off all my screens at least an hour before I go to bed.

Here's a little food for thought regarding limiting your screen time: Steve Jobs, the late co-founder and CEO of Apple, would not let his own kids use iPads. And his family had a phone-free dinner together every night. What did he know that the rest of us do not?

What about cigarettes, alcohol and drugs?

It seems that in the blue-collar trades, cigarettes, alcohol and sometimes drugs go hand-in-hand with blue-collar workers, especially for those of us who came up from working out in the field. If you grew up in a blue-collar family like I did, chances are you grew up seeing beer, cigarettes and maybe weed as a regular part of life.

When I was a kid I thought that smoking cigarettes was "what you're supposed to do," because everyone in my family smoked. I was conditioned to see smoking cigarettes as normal. I started smoking when I was 17 and smoked for about 11 years. Then in November 2006 my dad called me and said he had stage 4 lung cancer. For me that was it. I got that news and it was a simple, "I'm done." Dad died 14 months later at the age of 59.

Everyone knows that smoking can cause cancer. The American Lung Association says it contributes to 80 to 90% of lung cancer deaths and that men who smoke are 23 times more likely to develop lung cancer than those who don't smoke. But until it really hits home, it's easy to rationalize that everyone you know smokes and they're fine, so all those warnings are a bunch of bullshit.

I'm here to tell you that those warnings are *not* a bunch of bullshit!

How about alcohol? My dad also drank a lot, and I started bringing him beer out of the fridge when I was very young. Dad drank, all the men I knew drank, so naturally when I was 17, I started drinking, too – and my drinking continued for a long time.

It's no secret that drinking can be a slippery slope. Some people do okay with it. They have a few beers on the weekend. No big deal. But I've seen many blue-collar workers, myself included, start out small but then over time let it become more, more, more. Eventually it gets to the point where everything you do has to have a drink. Dinner has a drink. You have a good day at work, you stop by happy hour at your favorite bar to celebrate with a drink. You have a bad day at work, you have a drink to cheer yourself up. Everything becomes an excuse to drink.

The potential long-term health impacts from alcohol consumption include high blood pressure, heart disease, stroke, liver disease, digestive problems and dementia. The short-term negatives include impulsive behavior and lowered inhibitions (so you do stupid things), inability to maintain a good emotional state, inability to think clearly and, of course, hangovers.

The same goes for drugs, especially weed now that it's legal in much of the country. It often all starts off as social conditioning, recreational fun or curiosity because you were around it through your family or just society. "Okay," you think, "let's try something everyone says is fun." Then pretty soon it escalates. It was an occasional fun thing to do. Now it's a crutch, because now you're trying to self-medicate when something is wrong. You're getting high because you had a fight, lost your job, are pissed at your spouse, whatever. Then somewhere along the line it turns into a habit, and that habit becomes an addiction.

Everyone has a different thing. Some people love weed, beer, cigarettes or whisky (or all of the above). Some have an obsessive compulsive addiction to food. But that pattern of how people get from "giving it a try" to "addiction" applies to all these things that I'm calling "poisons."

All of that said, as someone who partied hard most of my life, I'm not preaching that you have to be all straight-edge. I'm not saying you can never have a drink or smoke a joint. I'm just speaking from experience as someone who took the partying lifestyle a little too far.

I've seen a lot of people who started off the same way I did and quickly blew way past "moderation" into "problem." And I've seen that the person who is addicted never believes that they've crossed the threshold of moderation until the shit gets really destructive and chaotic. Even then, sometimes bad stuff happens and the person *still* doesn't think there's a problem.

How do you tell what is "moderation" for you? If any of these substances are compromising your personal or professional life in any way, shape or form – even if it's just a tiny bit – pay attention. Most likely you're no longer in the "moderation" zone. Are these habits (i.e., addictions) causing you to be fat, lazy, angry, dumb, irritable, etc.? Do they model well for your children?

These habits or addictions around the things I'm calling poisons are often coping mechanisms for dealing with feelings. Ultimately, subconsciously and psychologically, everyone is looking for an emotional feeling. Personally, through my own experience in addressing my addiction, I realized that my drinking was my way of trying to "plug an emotional hole" that I felt deep inside.

If you find yourself highly attracted to and/or addicted to these vices, if you feel like you need something from the outside to help you feel better on the inside, recognize that this is really a Mindset pillar issue. If your experience is anything like mine, you may have some inner work that you need to do in the faith, spirituality and mindset aspect of life. I challenge you to consider making it a priority to work on this.

Remember, everything is connected, so all of the mindset stuff that we talked about in Chapters 4, 5 and 6 applies here in the Fitness pillar, too. In some cases, mindset issues are really at the core of the issues you are facing in one of the other pillars. As you put some energy into creating new, healthier habits, you'll probably find that doing so helps you build a different mindset in which you'll feel better and be better able to cope with certain situations, without the need to use outside substances in order to feel good.

Key Points for Chapter 9

- A healthy lifestyle includes *everything* related to how you treat or take care of your body, including diet, exercise, hydration, sleep, TV and screen time, "poisons" (cigarettes, alcohol and drugs) and mindset.

- Even if you have a physical job, you still need to exercise outside of work.

- A lot of common foods and food ingredients are not good for you.

- Hydration, sleep and screen time all have bigger impacts than you may realize.

- The use of cigarettes, alcohol and drugs, which is often a coping mechanism for dealing with feelings and/or internal issues and conflicts, can have serious negative health effects *and* can easily go from moderation to problem.

Chapter 9 Exercise

Self-awareness is always the first step towards change, so assess where you're currently at regarding all the elements of a healthy lifestyle. Be especially honest with yourself regarding whether you've gone past "moderation" and into "addiction" in your consumption of cigarettes, alcohol, drugs or even food.

If you're already doing well in some of these areas, great, give yourself a pat on the back. But if you see room for improvement, commit to making some changes.

CHAPTER 10:

IMPLEMENTING THE PRINCIPLES OF THE FITNESS PILLAR

Author Jim Rohn said, "Take care of your body. It's the only place you have to live in." Motivational speaker Denis Waitley said, "Time and health are two precious assets that we don't recognize and appreciate until they have been depleted." I agree with both of them.

While some people have to deal with medical conditions that are completely outside of their control (such as genetic diseases or things you are born with), most of us can have a great deal of command over whether we are healthy or ill. It's all about your habits and choices.

If you want to have the physical health and mental clarity necessary to be a leader and to enjoy an abundantly fulfilled lifestyle, the Fitness pillar is another place where being a change maker and habit creator is key.

Start with something small

If the Fitness pillar is your weakness, don't expect yourself to go from zero to hero in less than a week. Changing these habits takes time and determination, and if you keep expecting yourself to take an "all or nothing" approach you'll probably end up with nothing.

When I made the commitment to myself to lean into exercise I started *very* small. I joined a gym and committed to going once a week for 30 minutes each time. Just getting there was half the battle. That feeling of dread would come on the night before! "Oh, fuck, I have to go to the gym tomorrow," I'd think. But I made a commitment to myself to go, so I went. Once I showed up I didn't really do much. I'd do a little walking on the treadmill, lift some light weights and just hang out.

My goal was to break the mold and start a new pattern. I knew I wasn't going to get in shape with this exercise routine, but I had to start somewhere.

Gradually I started increasing my goal. I bumped things up to twice a week. Then I went from 30 minutes each time to an hour, which was pure hell for me. Like torture. But I did it. After about a year I went to three times a week, and so forth.

If exercise is a struggle, that's what I recommend you do, too. Start small and prove to yourself that you can make a commitment to do something and that you can break the pattern of your past behavior. It can be as small as a 5-minute daily walk. You just need to get started. Do that small step over and over for a few months without judgement or expectations or self-critiquing. Then find gratitude in the fact that you've broken the mold, even if you've just taken a very small step.

This also goes back to what you learned in Chapter 5: Your thoughts create your reality. If you've spent years telling yourself that you're not capable, your subconscious mind now believes that you're not capable and is acting accordingly. For me I eventually realized that the half-assed workout routine that I did for the first two years of this journey proved that "I'm not capable" was just a limiting belief. It was clearly not true.

Anyhow, once you've mastered that first small step, take another small step, and another, and another, and another. Eventually you'll get momentum in the process and get to a place where you feel much more confident about something that was previously a struggle. You'll overcome that limiting belief and start to reprogram your subconscious mind towards success.

A lot of people end up giving up on exercise because they try to do too much too soon. Instead of starting small and easing into it, they start big and fail. Then they see it as proof that they really can't do it. "I knew I was going to fail," they say. "I knew I couldn't do it, so F it. I'm not doing it." So it becomes a self-fulfilling prophecy.

Be aware that if you've always believed that you can't do it, your brain will be doing its best to prove that this is true. Don't get sucked into that trap! Instead, shut down any unhelpful thoughts or chatter in your head.

For example, when I first started going to the gym I was embarrassed. I was looking around at all these guys who are in awesome shape, and I just felt fat. I was certain that they were all laughing at me in their heads because I didn't belong there.

If you have these type of thoughts and these fears of being judged, too, you need to become aware of them and then focus your mind elsewhere. Maybe those other people at the gym *are* judging you. More likely they couldn't care less about you – they're just there to get their own workout in. Whatever. Either way, realize that it really doesn't matter. What matters is that you're there, and you're creating new patterns and habits for yourself.

It took me several *years* to create those new patterns and habits and get to where I wanted to be, but I got there. Today I work out five days a week. I no longer dread it. I just get up in the morning, head to the gym and do my thing. I still don't love exercising, but I do love how it makes me feel. I always feel amazing after I exercise! I feel proud, confident, invigorated. It catapults my day.

Get help

If the Fitness pillar is a struggle for you, don't try to go it alone. Get help.

When overcoming your weak pillar it's important to surround yourself with someone or multiple people who can help you. Lean on them when you're feeling down, and let them help pull you through those hard days.

For example, if you can afford it and it makes sense for you, hire a personal trainer. If not, reach out to a friend for assistance. Chances are there's someone in your network or community who is in good shape who can guide you. Or get an "accountability buddy" – someone who is in the same boat as you, who commits to working out with you. If you go to the gym long enough you can make friends with someone there who is in great shape.

There are even free Facebook groups for health and wellness that you can join, where you can ask questions, get tips and find support.

Figure out an exercise plan that works for you

What type of exercise should you do? Since there is no "one size fits all" answer here, you'll have to figure that out for yourself. But if fitness is your "kryptonite" and you're following the "start small" approach described above, the best way to get started is to find something that you know with utmost certainty that you can do *right now*. I don't care what kind of shape you're in, what can you do *right now*?

If going to the gym isn't your thing, find something fun you can do. Start playing pickleball or racquet ball. Join a softball league. Go for a hike. Find some empty floor space in your home and exercise along to some of the hundreds of free exercise videos available on YouTube. The important thing is that you find something you can do that raises your heart rate and requires you to exert physical energy.

If you have a physical job, review what I said in the last chapter about doing exercise that complements the exercise you get at work and helps you build the endurance to do those things.

Whatever you figure out is right for you, have a plan, write it down and commit to it. What will you do and how often will you do it? Then, over time, progressively increase the intensity of this plan until you have built up to what feels to you like a full exercise program.

Yes, you CAN do it! But you will have to stop believing your own lies that say otherwise.

Find and switch to a healthy diet that works for your body

There are a ton of different diets out there that all claim to be "healthy." There's the Mediterranean diet, the keto diet, the Atkins diet, the

Whole30 diet, low carb diets, raw food diets, vegetarian or vegan diets, blah, blah, blah and the list goes on and on.

Which one should you follow? I don't know. There is no one "right" answer here either. You need to educate yourself, use common sense and figure out what works for you and your life and body. Do your research, decide how much commitment you want to put into it and then do your best to fuel your body with foods that will support the life of abundance and fulfillment that you are creating.

What I don't recommend is that you follow one of the fad diets. Sure, people lose weight with the fad diets – but then they gain it all back again as soon as they stop the diet. What you need is a doable "permanent lifestyle change" diet. The idea is to take tiny steps in order to lose weight slowly and steadily, and then keep that weight off for the long haul.

Whatever diet you decide to follow, don't expect perfection. Unless you have a life-threatening food allergy or some other serious diet-related health condition, occasionally eating the "wrong" thing is not going to kill you.

Cut your intake of sugar and processed foods

If you're like most Americans, right now you're eating or drinking a total of about 17 teaspoons of added sugar each day. That's about 1/3 of a cup of sugar every single day! Where's all that sugar coming from? About half comes from sugary drinks. It's in your energy drink and your soda. It's in that sugar you add to your coffee. Depending on what type of alcohol you prefer, it may be there, too.

What about artificial sweeteners? Can't you just switch to Sweet'N Low®, Equal® or Splenda®? No. They're not exactly "health food" either. I read about a 2022 study that said drinking just one can of artificially-sweetened beverage per day makes you three times more likely to develop dementia or have a stroke. Is that what you want for yourself?

Start paying attention to all the sugar you're consuming, and then start reducing or eliminating these things from your diet. Because sugar is so addictive, you might have more long-term success if you do this gradually. Cut back from three cans of soda a day to two cans, and then go down to just one. Put less sugar in your coffee. Or, even better, get used to black coffee. Personally, I now like iced black coffee. Make things like cake, cookies and donuts an occasional treat instead of a daily thing. If you do this gradually, it will be easier to make the changes permanent.

Take the same approach to cutting processed foods out of your diet, too.

Drink enough water

At a minimum, every day you should drink half your body weight in ounces. So if you weigh 200 pounds you should drink 100 ounces of water every day. That's about 3/4 of a gallon. But that's a minimum. If you're out in the field sweating up a storm, drink more. If you're exercising, drink more. If your mouth feels dry, drink more.

If you're used to drinking soda and now the taste of water seems too boring to you, try adding some slices of lemon or cucumber or something like that. But watch out for those water flavor enhancers you see at the store, because those contain sweeteners.

I also recommend that you drink water first thing in the morning.

Before you go to bed, mix a high-quality salt electrolyte/hydration packet into a 12-ounce bottle of water, and put that on your nightstand. If you don't want to use one of those packets, you can also just mix in a few grains of pink Himalayan sea salt. Then when you wake up in the morning, start your day by chugging that water. This will give your body the electrolytes and hydration it needs so that all the cells and neurons in your brain can start firing the way they should.

Have a consistent bedtime and sleep routine

One of the things I've learned is that if you want to get enough sleep each night, having a consistent routine is key. For me, the more consistent I stay with the time I go to bed and the time I get up each morning, the better I sleep and feel.

I'm not at all a morning person, so in order to get the seven hours of sleep that I've found is my sweet spot, I aim to go to bed at 11:30 pm and wake up at 6:30 am each day. Most of the time I even stick with this schedule on the weekends. I've noticed that when I stay up late on Saturday night hanging with friends or watching a movie, just doing that one night on the weekend, it kind of screws me up. I don't feel as good the next day. And then the next night, when I try to go to bed at 11:30, it's like my brain won't want to shut down. "Hey!" the little voice in my head will scream, like a toddler who doesn't want to go to bed, "You stayed up late last night! I want to stay up late again now!"

Am I saying you need to go to bed at 11:30 pm and wake up at 6:30 am, too? Absolutely not! What's important here is consistency. You need to figure out what your body's natural circadian rhythm is and create a routine around that. If you're a night owl and you have the flexibility in your workday to be able to stay up until 1:00 am and get up at 8:00 am, go with it.

If you have the flexibility, it's also okay to take a little siesta or "cat-nap" in the afternoon. After all, historically, taking an afternoon nap or rest has been very common throughout much of the world. Maybe take 15 minutes during your lunch break to just give your body and mind a rest.

Avoid your TV, cell phone, computer and tablet before bed

Although it can be very difficult to do, something else that I highly recommend as part of your bedtime routine is to shut off your TV, cell phone, computer, tablet and any other screens at least 30 minutes (although 60 minutes is even better!) before bed. Between the blue light that screens put out and the stimulation that you get from active screen use, such as scrolling through your social media feeds, your screen time can make it difficult to get a good night's sleep.

CHAPTER 11:

UNDERSTANDING THE FINANCE PILLAR,
PART 1 – LEADERSHIP & STRUCTURE

The Finance Pillar is about how you make money. Which means we're going to delve deeply into what it takes to run a successful service business in the trades. Yes, this is the business tactics, tools and structure information that you thought was all you needed, before I hit you with all of that "life" stuff in Chapters 1 through 10!

For most of the business owners I work with, this information is nearly all new. Most started as a technician like I did and ended up running a business, without having had any formal education in how to do this. It might all be new to you, too. All I can say is I sure wish I had learned this stuff when I started my business, rather than much later after years of struggling with some wild ups and downs.

So buckle up, because the next few chapters are going to cover a lot of ground!

Successful businesses attract, deliver and retain

The first thing you need to wrap your head around regarding the mindset of running a business is the high-level concept of what your business does. And what all businesses must do to be successful is to attract, deliver and retain both internal and external customers. Your "internal customers" are your employees, while your "external customers" are the people and businesses that buy things from you.

As a business leader, these are the three high-level things you must focus on: attract, deliver and retain. If you do not successfully do these three things, your business will not make money. In practical terms this means that you and your leadership team need to build out systems, processes and procedures for attracting, delivering and retaining employees and customers.

On the employee side this means mapping out and formalizing your answers to some basic questions, including:

- **How do we attract employees?** What are we doing to attract high-quality employees to our business?

- **How do we deliver the training and development that our employees need** to be successful at their jobs?

- **What do we do to retain our employees?** How do we give our employees a career path?

  Are we keeping them happy through culture, leadership, camaraderie, recognition, raises, incentives, etc.?

Of course, you also need to go through this exercise on the external customers side, mapping out and formalizing standard operating procedures for all the following and more:

- **How do we attract new clients?** What are the systems and procedures for our sales and marketing processes? How do we measure the success of our marketing efforts? What exactly is each salesperson accountable for?

- **How do we deliver our operational services to our clients?** How do we handle incoming calls? How do we manage the dispatch process? How do we show up on site? How do we finish the service call? How do we invoice?

- **How do we retain clients?** How do we handle quality assurance and quality control? How often is someone reaching out to each client, and who is responsible for doing this?

A big mistake that a lot of business owners make is to only focus on the "attract clients" part of this process. They think the name of the game is to get more and more clients. But it doesn't do you any good to attract clients if you can't deliver the services that they're paying for. Your company will never grow – and it will most likely fail – if none of your first-time customers turn into on-going customers. Of course, there's also no point in attracting employees if they all quit after the first three months.

Attract, deliver, retain. You must do all three.

Embrace your role as the leader

I'll be honest. Leadership is not for the faint of heart. It takes a lot to lead a company, and the skills required may or may not come naturally to you. However, for the business to be successful you must embrace your role as the leader – whether you are leading the entire company or just a portion of it.

You also must develop excellent leadership skills. While this may seem obvious, it needs to be said anyway. If you're not a good leader, no one will follow you. You won't attract people to your business. You won't get any forward motion. Nothing will work consistently and sustainably.

What does it take to lead? What are the characteristics and actions of a good leader? There are literally thousands of books on leadership out there that all attempt to answer these questions. Don't worry if you haven't read them! For now, as you are learning the principles laid out in this Blueprint for Success, the following list is all you need…

Characteristics of effective leaders

Effective leaders are or have:

- **Vision and foresight** – As a leader you need to have a vision of where you want to take things, and the foresight to look at what's going on today to see what type of result this is likely to produce for tomorrow. Staying one step ahead makes it possible for you to compare the current path to the desired path and course correct as necessary.

- **Humble and self-aware** – If you're like most bosses/leaders/owners, you're hyper-concerned about your employees' performance. You constantly look at what others are doing right and wrong. But then you forget to look in the mirror and say, "What about me? What am I doing well? What do I suck at? What do I need to improve?"

  Being a humble and self-aware leader will get you really, really far in terms of other humans trusting you. When your team sees that you're not just coaching others and giving feedback – that you're open to being on the receiving end, too – this builds trust. Don't let your ego get in the way of humility and self-awareness.

Self-awareness is also the first step in personal development, so it's really an important trait for a leader to have.

- **Honest** – As you learned in Chapter 2, truth and integrity are the absolute values upon which the entire foundation of the Blueprint for Success is built. You must be honest with yourself and others. Everything you do as a leader must hinge or revolve around truth. You can't lie, bullshit or sugarcoat – that "fake it till you make it" game has a short shelf life. No one wants to follow someone who is manipulative or shady.

- **Self-confident** – If you're not confident in your own abilities, you'll never get others to be confident in theirs, or to believe in and follow you. Where does confidence come from? Ultimately, self-confidence comes from the promises that you keep with yourself. As I said in Chapter 2, self-confidence comes from living a life of truth and integrity, especially the integrity that you have with yourself. Once you have this foundation, your self-confidence will grow as your personal wisdom and experiences grow.

- **Consistent** – Do you know what happens if you keep changing the strategy and the way your company does things? People get frustrated and confused and start to hate their jobs. They also start to think that you don't know what the hell you're doing, so they stop trusting you.

The way to avoid this is to be hyper-consistent as a leader. Instead of constantly changing things, spend a lot of time thinking about vision and tactics *before* you implement anything. That way instead of needing to make the type of wholesale changes that drive everyone around you crazy, you'll be able to simply make minor course corrections that they can easily deal with.

- **Gritty** – Back in Chapter 4 I said that leaders must have a high level of grit, mental toughness and self-discipline. Then in Chapter 6 I provided some advice on how to increase your level of grit and self-discipline. Why is this so important? Because stuff happens. When it does, you need to be able to quickly regroup your emotions, mindset and spirit and get right back in the game. People are depending on you. They're trusting you to lead them. You need to have the grit to do so!

- **Emotionally intelligent** – We talked a lot about EQ (emotional intelligence) in Chapter 4. As a leader you need to have a high EQ. You need to have control of your emotional states, because in order to lead people you must be able to navigate issues, problems and adversity with a cool head. Successful leaders have the ability to remain calm under fire. If you respond to every situation by getting all fired up and triggered, no one will trust you or want to follow you.

    The good news is that you can evolve, change and improve your EQ. There are tools in Chapter 6 to help you do so.

- **Empathetic** – To be an effective leader you need to have empathy. You need to be able to feel and understand, or at least seek to understand, what others have to say and what they're feeling. You need to be open to navigating others' perspectives, even if you don't fully agree with them.

- **Ownership mindset** – Being the leader means taking ownership of everything in your world. Let go of the idea of finding someone to blame for a problem or issue. That doesn't matter. Your job is to find the answers to the following questions: How did this problem happen? How can we fix it? How can we prevent it from happening again?

That's it. Own everything. Solve, fix, prevent – all without any finger pointing, drama or animosity.

When you are an effective leader, everything is your fault and your problem, regardless of who else might be involved.

- **"Silver lining" mindset** – As a leader you need to think in terms of seeing the gift or lesson in every challenge or situation. You have to almost be grateful or thankful for challenges, struggles and breakdowns, knowing that each one comes with a lesson you can learn.

You need to embrace a mindset that you have to struggle well, and the bigger the struggle, the greater the potential reward.

Here's a little formula to keep in mind: If you embrace your struggles and learn how to reflect on problems and situations, and accept the fact that pain and discomfort is part of the game, then you'll be a person who grows and progresses in life as a leader.

Actions of effective leaders

Effective leaders:

- **Establish core values** – As we've discussed before, your core values are the guidelines for how you operate. Everything hinges on your company's core values. You lead, coach, discipline and reward by them. In Chapter 14 I provide advice on how to keep these core values front and center in everything you do.

- **Deliver results** – Your job is to make things happen and produce measurable, quantifiable results. To be a results-based leader you must know how to manage by the numbers. In Chapter 12 we'll get into how to do that.

- **Coach** – Leadership is a coaching game. It is important in leadership that you have the ability and confidence to quickly coach people up or out.

  That said, if someone is not being responsive to your leadership, the first place you need to look is at yourself. What do you need to change in order to get them to respond to your leadership? Is the employee's issue a skills issue or a willpower issue? If it's skills, than fixing this is 100% on you as the leader. You need to fully train and coach them to do the job successfully. And you need to be patient with the process, knowing that even with consistent coaching it takes 90 days or more to implement new habits.

  But if the problem is the employee's own laziness, negligence, dishonesty or whatever, then that's on them. It's your job to identify people who don't align, but it's not your job to fix them.

  Coach them up in the organization, or quickly coach them out the door.

- **Delegate** – A big key to delivering results is to become a delegation expert. You absolutely cannot have an attitude of, "If I want it done right I must do it myself." That is counterproductive, because leadership is about "we," not "me." Teach others the process. Give them simple instructions. Coach them on how to be effective. And then *let them do it!*

- **Hold the line** – Closely related to coaching and delegating is the ability to guide people and keep them aligned to the mission, policies and procedures. Human beings tend to "wiggle." They don't just naturally go where they're supposed to go. That's why this thing called "leadership" is required!

  Remember, it's not what you preach or teach as a leader that is ultimately reflected in your team's behavior. It's what you tolerate. That's what you're training people to do. No matter what you preach or teach, if you regularly tolerate deviations from the line, that's what you are going to get.

- **Be firm but fair** – How you talk to people is important. When communicating with your team you need to be firm but fair. Be consistent, and don't be too harsh or too soft.

- **Evolve** – Leadership is a journey, not a destination. To lead other people and grow a business you must constantly be on a path of expansion (which, of course, is what much of this book is about). There's a direct relationship between your team's rate of growth and your own rate of growth. You won't be able to help others grow if you're not growing yourself.

Get a management team in place

For the first 10 to 12 years of my business I had no concept of any type of an organizational structure. I simply wore a whole lot of hats. I was the manager of everything and everyone reported to me. I was in charge of sales, the service team, the field operations team, dispatch, accounting/finance, everything.

Like many entrepreneurs I was operating from a fear and scarcity mindset, so I was afraid to make the investment to bring in a manager or supervisor (or two or three), or train up a manager or supervisor. I would have to pay someone's salary, and I thought I couldn't afford it.

If I could go back in time I would have done things very differently, and that is my advice to you.

Your business has four main departments:

1. Operations

2. Customer Service

3. Sales and Marketing

4. Accounting and Finance

When you put a manager or supervisor in charge of each of these departments – someone who specializes in that business function and is totally on board with your business' core values – good things start to happen. First, your business becomes more manageable. For you personally everything becomes more fun and less stressful because now you're not trying to wear a stack of hats. Second, your business becomes much more scalable, which means you will find it easier to attract the additional work that is needed to support the salaries of these managers.

Here's another way to look at this. In the study of economics there's this concept called "opportunity cost." When you need to choose between alternatives, opportunity cost refers to the value of the thing you chose not to do. In other words, what is it costing you to *not* have managers in place? What opportunities are you missing out on because you're trying to do it all yourself?

Looking back at my own situation, I now realize that trying to do it all myself was so inefficient that I was missing out on sales, growth, training and development opportunities. I was holding the business back, and the lost business could have paid for the managers I desperately needed.

Don't make this mistake. As quickly as possible, and probably to the point where it feels uncomfortable, get at least a supervisor-level person in place to manage each of the four major departments of your business. Do this ASAP, "9-1-1" status!

The difference between leaders and managers

As you are putting a management team in place, it is important that you understand the difference between leaders and managers, so that you can get the right people in each position. Although they are often done by one person, I believe that "leadership" and "management" are two different things:

- **Leaders are the visionaries.** Leaders set the goals, create the plans and drive the energy. Leadership is about getting the right people together, laying out the mission/strategy/goals/objectives, getting everyone excited about these things and then motivating them to start moving towards making these things happen.

Leaders are the ones who have the "big picture" vision for where the business should go. Leaders are very effective at explaining the "3 whys" of the plan: why it's good for the customers, good for the business and good for the individual team members. This is important, because until people understand these whys, especially the "what's in it for me" factor, their motivation to move towards your desired outcome will be very low.

- **Managers are the integrators.** They're the doers who implement the plans. Managers understand each team member's strengths and weaknesses, set each person up for success based on these strengths and weaknesses, and then constantly monitor the team on an hourly and daily basis in order to do what it takes to keep each person on task.

  Managers have a great deal of patience and are typically very good at paying attention to details. They have the tenacity to be highly repetitive and redundant, constantly and consistently giving people feedback and redirecting them to where they should be and what they should be doing.

Some people are better at leading and some are better at managing. Personally, I *love* leadership! I believe that God put me on this planet to be a leader. But He did not put me on this planet with any management skills whatsoever. I am definitely not gifted with those. I get frustrated and turn into an asshole, and then people quit. Although I've developed management skills and can do it now, it certainly is not my passion.

For a long time I attempted to do both leadership and management. Once I was trained and understood the concept of leader/visionary versus manager/integrator, I realized that my poor management skills were holding my company back. This understanding allowed me to scale my business by finding others who are good at management and delegating these tasks to them.

The reality is, if you put a visionary leadership type of person in too much of a managerial role, they'll burn down your employees. These people don't have the right mindset for management and they don't have the EQ set to be consistent with what it takes to manage people.

Likewise, if you put a manager/integrator into the leader/visionary role, the team or business will hit a ceiling. Quite often the person who has the manager/integrator mindset doesn't see strategic opportunity. So the business will stay on course, but it won't evolve and grow because it will keep doing the same things it's been doing over and over again.

It's in the marriage of the leader/visionary with the manager/integrator that the magic happens. This is why bigger companies typically have a CEO (Chief Executive Officer), who is the leader/visionary, and a COO (Chief Operating Officer), who is the manager/integrator.

Accountability chart vs. organizational chart

As you get the right people in place, there are two common types of charts that you can use to represent the organizational structure of your business. The most common is the traditional organizational chart, often called an "org chart." An org chart shows the flow of who reports to who. Generally speaking, an org chart only shows the company's management, with each person's name and title listed in one of the boxes on the chart.

Although it is less common, my personal preference is an accountability chart, because it is laid out based on functions and roles. It's all well and good to know that someone is the Office Operations Manager, for example, but what is that person accountable for? What exactly do they do?

An accountability chart shows the three to five functions *and* three to five Key Performance Indicator (KPI) metrics that each person is accountable for. KPIs are quantifiable measurements of performance for specific objectives, such as the total dollar value of new maintenance contracts per month or the total number of new clients per month.

An accountability chart is therefore like an organizational chart on steroids, because it is more actionable, measurable and results-based. You can quickly see who is responsible for what, and the objective measurements on which each person's performance will be measured. It's a model that eliminates drama and room for interpretation, and provides a clear "line of sight" at the front end of how you run the business and the expectations of what each person on the team will accomplish.

If you are going to use an accountability chart, it's important that everyone on the team understands that they are *fully accountable* for delivering on these roles and metrics. They have to do whatever they need to do to make these things happen. If they have people who report to them, they need to ensure these direct reports' responsibilities also support making these things happen.

For example, say your company has an order to put 10 new air conditioning units on a building. If you are the Field Operations Manager in charge of that job, you are 100% accountable for every single thing that goes on in that project, both good and bad. You will have Installation Techs reporting to you, and you will structure the job so that each of these Techs has responsibilities and tasks that are appropriate for their roles. You will also work with your company's buyer to ensure all parts and materials are purchased, work with the dispatch department to schedule manpower, keep the sales rep who is ultimately in charge of the sales relationship with the client in the loop and so forth. Even though lots of people are involved, as the leader *you* have 100% accountability to oversee all aspects of the project and ensure it goes well, and meets the budget, profit goals and timeline.

Your Vision Execution Map (a.k.a. Strategic Plan)

When you are building and growing a business it is important that you have a Strategic Plan. I like to call this plan your "Vision Execution Map," because it lays out your vision for your business and provides a roadmap for making this vision a reality.

Once you have this dialed in, be sure to share it with your team! You'll get better results and higher morale if everyone knows where you're going and why, as well as how you're going to get there.

Here are the major components of your Vision Execution Map:

Big Hairy Audacious Goal (BHAG) – This is your big, crazy, "straight shot for the moon" goal of where you want your business to be in terms of revenue 20 years from now. This should be a goal that's so big it makes you feel uncomfortable.

Core Things About Your Business – These are things that define what your business is all about:

• Core values

• Mission statement

• Purpose statement

• Secret sauce

The "secret sauce" is the market differentiator that makes your company different and better than others, such as your training systems, culture or service delivery. Why should people buy from you vs. anyone else? Why should they work for you vs. anyone else?

10-Year Target – At the high level, where do you see your business in 10 years? Your 10-Year Target should include:

- Top line total revenue

- Net profit

- Number of employees

- Products/services/divisions

- Market sectors that you're serving

- Geographic areas that you're working in

3-Year Plan – This gets more granular than the 10-Year Target. Your 3-Year Plan should include:

- Top line total revenue

- Revenue and gross profit margin by division, such as Service, Maintenance and Retrofit/Replacement work

- Net profit

- Number of employees

- Accountability chart showing the people you will need in order to reach and support your revenue goals (i.e., managers, supervisors, sales reps, dispatchers, technicians, buyers, accountants, bookkeepers, etc.)

- Market sectors that you're serving

- Geographic areas that you're working in

1-Year Expectation – This is the most granular part of your Vision Execution Map. Your 1-Year Expectation shows a 1-year version of all the items that are in the 3-Year Plan *plus more details*. These additional details include:

- Minimum expectations for revenue, gross profit margin and net profit for each month of the year (if your business has "busy" and "slow" seasons, be sure to account for this in these month-to-month numbers)

- List of the big action items and strategic initiatives that you need to do, broken out by quarter and department

  o These initiatives are things that optimize and evolve the business, that move the business forward, not just things that people do as part of their regular job. This can include everything from operational initiatives to marketing or whatever. These initiatives should be overarching things that need to get done to "work *on* the business" vs. "work *in* the business."

  o Each strategic initiative must be owned by only ONE person.

When looking at what you want to see happen in the next year, don't make the mistake of just looking at total revenue. In this time frame it's much more important to look at ways to make this revenue along the way – the cash flow and profits that are needed for your business to scale and sustain. That's why all of those monthly numbers are critical indicators. If you're not hitting these minimum expectation targets, you'll never hit your total revenue goal.

A big key here is that you need to make sure that what you're doing in the 1-year timeframe will roll up into your 3-Year Plan. If you take the 3-year target and divide it into thirds, can you see where you're at now scaling up into that 3-year target? If not, are you either being overly optimistic with your 3-year target or setting the bar too low?

Quarterly Expectation – As humans we're flowing in minutes, hours, days, weeks and months. But because of the laws of momentum in a business, it is really hard to implement a change and see beneficial results in less than 90 days. As a leader you must be mindful that regardless of how hard you push change upon your business, it will take about 90 days to see the impact of your efforts.

This is why you need to take your 1-Year Expectations and chop it into fourths. Then each quarter do a high-level analysis on where you went – the actual vs. the expectation – and make any necessary adjustments in real time.

Key Points for Chapter 11

- Successful businesses attract, deliver and retain employees and customers.

- Getting the right leadership team in place, and ensuring that you are tracking and measuring the three to five key functions (KPIs) that each employee or leader is accountable for, is crucial.

- You need to have a vision and a plan (your Vision Execution Map) for how you will turn this vision into reality.

Chapter 11 Exercise

Now is the time for reflection. Take some thinking time to do a deep-level assessment of everything in your business. Look at all the departments and employees. What is or is not working? In terms of your people, who is or is not working? Think about yourself as the leader and/or business owner. What do you love about what you're doing? What needs to be delegated? Get out a journal and get some good notes down from all of this.

This reflection and assessment will be super helpful as you move forward with implementing systems, structures and tactics to get your business running well.

CHAPTER 12:

UNDERSTANDING THE FINANCE PILLAR,
PART 2 – FINANCIAL & OPERATIONAL METRICS

The way a business makes money is that it turns assets into sales, turns sales into profits and then turns profits into cash. You buy assets, such as equipment and vehicles. You employ people who can help you attract, deliver and retain internal and external customers. You deliver the goods and services that you sell. Then you take the money that comes in from this and use it to pay for all the costs associated with running your business. The money that is left then needs to be carefully and wisely used and stored in order to fund your business' ongoing operations and growth.

Your financial and operational reports and metrics give you invaluable insight into how you are doing in this quest to turn assets into sales, sales into profits and profits into cash.

Before you keep reading, I recommend that you take a few minutes *right now* and print out copies of your company's Profit and Loss Statement, Balance Sheet and Statement of Cash Flows. I am going to be talking about how to understand these reports, and it would be super-helpful if you had the ones for your company in front of you as you follow along.

If you are an employee and do not have access to your employer's financial reports, look for generic sample reports online.

The three most important financial reports

There are three major financial reports that come out of your accounting software: the Profit and Loss Statement (also called your "P&L" or "Income Statement"), the Balance Sheet and the Statement of Cash Flows (also called your "Cash Flow Statement").

The Profit and Loss Statement and Statement of Cash Flows each look at a user-selected period of time. These both have a start date and a finish date. In contrast, the Balance Sheet is a snapshot in time of numbers that start at the inception of the company and keep going indefinitely until the business is closed.

You should have your entire accounting system – and therefore all three of these reports – set up on an "accrual basis" rather than a "cash basis." "Accrual basis" means that you record revenue and expenses in the time period in which you create the invoice or get the bill. "Cash basis" means that you record revenue and expenses when you receive the money or pay the bill, which can be much later than when the invoice was created or the bill was received.

Unless you enjoy failing, doing things the hard way and/or burning through a shitload of money, as a business owner it's highly, highly important that you learn how to read and understand all three of your key financial reports. It is also vitally important that you actually review these reports at least once a week to see how they are trending. At the absolutely worst case – which I *don't* recommend – review them once a month. It is really bad if you only look at them every few months, because a lot can go wrong while you're not paying attention.

To be successful in business you *must* have financial literacy. At a minimum, that means learning how to understand these three financial reports.

Understanding your Profit and Loss Statement

Your Profit and Loss Statement shows you all the sales you made and costs you incurred during a specified period of time. Let's take a look at the main line items on this report...

- **Total Income** (also known as "Revenue") – This is obvious. It's the dollar value of the sales you made during the given time period.

- **Direct Costs** – Also known as Cost of Goods Sold ("COGS"), direct costs are things that can be allocated directly to a job number or work order. These are the costs of all the things you put on the job out in the field, such as materials, contractors, vendors and equipment rentals. These things are called "direct material expenses." The other piece of this is direct labor, the money you pay to your field staff plus all the costs associated with having these employees.

  Remember, if you're paying someone $35 an hour, it costs you a lot more than $35 an hour to have this person on your payroll. By the time you add in state taxes, federal taxes, workers compensation insurance, medical benefits, vacation pay, holiday pay, training, etc., your total cost of employing this person is probably $70 an hour. In fact, a good (but not perfect) rule of thumb is that your fully loaded labor cost is probably double the person's hourly rate.

- **Indirect Costs** – Indirect costs are costs that exist because of your field team, that cannot be directly allocated to a job or work order number. Examples of indirect costs are your monthly fuel bill, technician uniforms and cell phones, vehicle-related costs (including payments) and the costs associated with training your technicians.

- **Gross Profit** – Your income minus your direct and indirect costs is your gross profit. This is how much money you make on your job, work order or service call, *after* you have collected the money from the client and paid all your vendors or suppliers, indirect costs and field employees who did the work.

- **Gross Margin** – Gross margin is your gross profit expressed as a percentage of your total income or sales. If you've got $50,000 in gross profit and $100,000 in sales, your gross margin is 50%. Note that the gross margin may not be listed on your P&L Statement – you may need to calculate it yourself.

  For the service side of your business, you should be targeting at least 50% gross margin, and shooting for 55 to 60% gross margin. For equipment installations, replacements and retrofits you should ideally be targeting a 40 to 45% gross margin – and accept as a standard no less than 35 to 38% gross margin.

- **Sales & Marketing** – For a service-based business you should aim to keep your sales and marketing costs at 8 to 10% of revenue.

- **Overhead** – Overhead, which may be labeled "Expense" or "G&A" (General & Administrative) on your P&L Statement, includes all the costs related to running a business that are *not* allocated to your direct or indirect field costs or your sales and marketing costs.

  Overhead includes rent or mortgage and other building-related expenses, utilities, insurance, your non-field staff and support staff (dispatch, accounting and finance, managers), telephone system, computer system, utilities, property insurance, general liability insurance, office supplies and expenses, purchases of small office equipment (such as printers), etc. For a service-based business you should aim to keep your overhead at 18 to 22% or less of revenue.

  Here's a simple way to understand your costs. Costs that happen in the field are Direct Costs and Indirect Costs. Costs happening in your office are Overhead/G&A.

- **Net Profit** – Also called "Net Income" or "EBITDA" (Earnings Before Interest, Taxes, Depreciation and Amortization), your net profit is what's left of your income *after* you have paid all your direct, indirect, sales and marketing and overhead costs. If you look at your net profit as a percentage of your sales, ideally this should be a minimum of 15 to 18%. A higher net profit rate than this is, of course, even better.

A big thing that all of this tells you is whether or not you're really making money, how much you're making and if the amount you're making is something to celebrate or something that needs significant improvement. If your net profit is much lower than it should be, your P&L Statement also shows you exactly how you spent or allocated your revenue, to help you see where the problem is.

But if you don't know how to read and interpret this report – or if you know but never bother to look at this report, or you don't have this report functioning or set up – you'll be in the dark.

Understanding your Balance Sheet

Your Balance Sheet shows you what you own ("assets"), what you owe ("liabilities") and how much equity you have at a specific point in time. "Equity" is money that's been put into the business either by you as the owner or by an investor.

Your Balance Sheet is based on a simple mathematical formula:

$$Equity = Assets - Liabilities$$

Your P&L Statement is all about your company's profits, which is super important. But a lot of people make the mistake of thinking that "profits" = "cash." They're wrong. Profit is *not* cash. Profit is a concept, a math theory. And "cash" is not necessarily what you have in the bank. Cash is what you own or have *after* you pay your debts.

If you have $500,000 in the bank and $400,000 of debts (also known as "liabilities"), you do not have $500,000 in cash. You have $100,000 in cash. There's a big difference! This can fool you if you don't know how to read a balance sheet.

The main components of a Balance Sheet are:

• **Assets**

    o **Current Assets** – These are assets that are expected to be converted into cash or used up within one year. For example: cash, cash equivalents, short-term investments, accounts receivable and inventory.

o **Non-Current Assets** – These are long-term assets that are expected to provide benefits beyond one year. Non-current assets include property, plant and equipment ("PP&E"); intangible assets such as patents, copyrights and an accounting concept called "goodwill"; and long-term investments.

- **Liabilities**

   o **Current Liabilities** – This is debt that you need to pay off within one year, such as your accounts payable, short-term loans and other short-term financial obligations.

   o **Non-Current Liabilities** – This is debt and other obligations with due dates that extend beyond one year. This can include long-term debt, deferred tax liabilities and long-term lease obligations.

- **Equity**

   o **Common Stock** – This represents ownership in the company, even if the company is privately owned and the stock is not available for sale.

   o **Retained Earnings** – This is the accumulated net income that has been kept in the company over time rather than distributed to shareholders as dividends.

   o **Other Equity Items** – This can include other comprehensive income and equity from non-controlling interests.

Your Balance Sheet tells you what you're doing with your money. How much money do you have in the bank? How much money is owed to you in terms of your accounts receivable or any money that your business loaned out to others? If you own buildings, vehicles or equipment, what are these assets worth?

How are you paying for assets, like vehicles or large equipment? Who do you owe money to in terms of your accounts payable, or money owed on vehicle loans or loans you took out to run the business?

If you only know how to read a Profit and Loss Statement, you're better off than most business owners I talk to. But if you don't also know how to read a Balance Sheet, you're still flying the plane somewhat blind, and you're likely to get yourself in trouble.

Understanding your Statement of Cash Flows

Money comes into your business after you do the work, bill the customer and then collect the money through your accounts receivable. Ideally you will collect *all* the money that is owed to you. However, anyone who extends credit to their customers knows that you don't always collect all your money, and when you do collect it, the money does not always come in as quickly as you would like it to.

The Statement of Cash Flows is a more detailed view of how you spent the money that came in during a particular period in time. Are you investing it? Using it for operations? Using it to buy assets to grow the business? Taking money out to pay dividends or distributions to yourself as the business owner?

At the simple level, your Statement of Cash Flows essentially answers these three questions:

1. How much cash came in during this time period?

2. How much cash did you spend during this time period, and what did you spend it on?

3. How much cash was left at the end of the time period?

At the higher level, your Statement of Cash Flows helps you understand your business' liquidity, meaning your ability to meet your short-term and long-term financial obligations. How much cash does your business need to operate right now? This report can also show you if your business is generating enough cash to fund your desired growth.

The main components of your Statement of Cash Flows are:

- **Operating Activities** – This shows how the company's core business activities generate and use cash.

  o **Inflows** – Cash coming in, mainly from sales of goods or services, and, potentially, other operating receipts.

  o **Outflows** – Payments to suppliers, employees, government (taxes) and others for operating costs.

- **Investing Activities** – By showing where the company's investments are made, investing activities can signal the company's strategy and future earning capacity.

  o **Inflows** – In this section, inflows mainly come from sales of long-term assets, such as securities or property, plant and equipment.

  o **Outflows** – This is related to acquisitions of long-term assets and investments.

- **Financing Activities** – Here you can see how the company sources and repays capital, which affects its capital structure and dividend policy.

  o **Inflows** – This could be from issuing new debt or equity.

o **Outflows** – This includes debt repayments, dividend payments and buybacks of the company's own shares.

- **Free Cash Flow (FCF)** – Free Cash Flow is essentially the net effect or result of how cash is used or spent in your organization. It is calculated as follows:

Free Cash Flow = Cash Flow from Operating Activities – Capital Expenditures

Free cash flow shows the discretionary cash that is available after funding the company's operating activities and capital expenditures. Free cash flow can be used for things like paying dividends or investing in growth opportunities.

Free cash flow is super important because it is an essential metric for understanding the company's financial health and flexibility.

Invest wisely

As I said earlier, the way a business makes money is it turns assets into sales, turns sales into profits and then turns profits into cash. The art of the game is therefore to become an expert at taking assets (i.e., things and stuff) and making the most amount of profit you can with it, and then turning that profit into free cash flow. Doing this means spending your investment cash wisely.

Pay attention to whether a proposed investment is a "need" or a "want." Do you really *need* that item, or is it just a new "toy" that you *want*? You must be strategic about your business investments.

For example, a good investment is to ensure your work vehicles are properly stocked so that you're sending your technicians into the field with all the tools, equipment and inventory they are likely to need to do their job. This will make your technicians more efficient and effective, which will not only bring in more profits but will also be good for morale and employee retention.

On the other hand, buying a new forklift, work truck, building or whatever does not automatically guarantee that you'll create enough additional sales from these new assets to make a profit on your investment. It only means that you'll have more assets, and you'll have the costs associated with paying for and managing these assets. You need to carefully analyze the likely impact that a proposed investment will have on your business.

Leading indicators vs. lagging indicators

The three financial reports we just discussed are vitally important parts of your business intelligence and financial literacy. All three provide what's called "lagging indicators," meaning they are history reports. You're looking in the rear view mirror of your business. While it's highly valuable information, these reports show you things that have already happened. The month/quarter/year has already passed, and there's nothing you can do today to change any of the numbers being reported.

Another type of indicator that you should be looking at is what's called "leading indicators." These are the KPIs (Key Performance Indicators or, as I like to call them, Kept Promise Indicators) that you establish as part of your Accountability Chart. Leading indicators measure things that are happening today that can help you predict if you will meet your business goals tomorrow, next week, next month, etc.

The KPIs measure the daily and weekly behaviors that individuals within your organization need to have. If achieved, these behaviors produce a desired outcome which will help ensure the company reaches its financial goals, which will then be reflected in the financial reports.

You need to establish and track KPIs for each major function and each leader or manager in your business. These KPIs should then be listed on your Accountability Chart. Your managers, in turn, need to establish and track KPIs for each of their direct reports.

For example, think of your service team. One of your goals for your service team is to bill as much of your techs' time as possible. Ideally for every hour that you pay your tech you will also bill a client for one hour (or more!) of that tech's time. The KPI that tracks this is what's called your "technician utilization rate" or "production efficiency rate." This is the ratio of hours billed vs. hours paid. Your goal is for this to be 1 to 1, or a 100% rate or better. From the production standpoint, 80% is the absolute minimum I recommend – and this is only acceptable on a temporary basis since it means that for every 8 hours billed, you're paying out 10 hours to your technician. This is a great way to go broke!

To get a full view of what is going on in your business, you should be using both leading and lagging indicators.

Scorecards, scoreboards and dashboards

Scorecards, scoreboards and dashboards are what give you this full view of your leading and lagging indicators. The idea here is to constantly have data in your face so you can keep the organization performing properly, course correcting any issues before things get too far off track.

• **Job Scorecards** are at the employee level. A job scorecard is a high-performance version of a job description. This tells the employee, in bullet point format, what they own. The Job Scorecard should show accountabilities and responsibilities; behavioral expectations; the employee's daily, weekly and monthly "must do" tasks; and the KPIs on which they will be measured.

Look to have just three to five simple KPIs for each person. These should be mathematically easy to measure, based on data that is readily available from your systems.

- **Departmental Scoreboards** show a sum of the KPIs for each employee in that department. For example, say you have 10 sales reps and each sales rep is measured on four KPIs: cold calls, appointments, proposals and sales. The Departmental Scoreboard would show the total cold calls, appointments, proposals and sales made by these 10 sales reps.

Ideally you should have three to five KPIs per person and three to five (but at most seven) KPIs per department – and often these will overlap. Whatever these KPIs are, you must have *one* person who is 100% accountable for these departmental results. This person, of course, will have people who report to them who will help produce those outcomes. If multiple people are responsible, instead of results you'll get animosity, finger pointing and blame.

Because you should have one Departmental Scoreboard for each department, you will most likely have four Departmental Scoreboards: Operations, Customer Service, Sales & Marketing and Accounting & Finance. You can even put these on a spreadsheet or in software that will allow you to see all of them at once.

You *must* review these once a week. Period!

- **CEO Dashboards** are designed to give the owner or top executive a high-level view of the business. The CEO Dashboard should include:

  o The results shown on the Scoreboards for each department

  o Average revenue per employee

  o Average KPIs for your technicians

  o The sales team's closing ratios vs. expectation

  o All of your important financial report indicators, such as sales and margin by department, net profit, some balance sheet ratios and more

  o Results of employee and customer satisfaction surveys

  o Any other critical things for the business that do not directly relate to a department, that the owner or top executive is accountable for

You *must* review this once a week. Period!

Meeting rhythm and structure

It is important to set up meetings correctly in a business, because getting this right is a vital part of implementing and achieving what you have laid out in your Vision Execution Map. The point of meetings is to assess where things are, resolve issues, determine actions to be taken and recognize results. Being able to properly tackle these "assess, resolve, execute, recognize" steps requires a certain amount of touch with your people.

In establishing a meeting rhythm, your goal is to hit the perfect balance of meeting often enough to accomplish your goals but not so often that you're just wasting everyone's time. And you want to ensure that your meetings are very structured, with formal meeting times and very formal, structured agendas. Otherwise things will go off into unproductive, emotional dialogue.

The following is a highly-developed meeting rhythm and structure that has proven to be very successful for my business.

Annual – 1 Day – Owner, Leadership Team

- Create and update Vision Execution Map

- Update 1-Year Expectation, including review of financial results

- Review CEO Dashboard and Departmental Scoreboards

- Review results of major action items and minor to do items ("Majors and Minors") by quarter

Quarterly – 4 to 8 hours – Owner, Leadership Team

- Review Vision Execution Map & previous quarter's Major & Minor Action Items

- Set 3 Majors & 6 Minors per quarter (but not more than this) per person / leader

- Complete last quarter's missed Majors & Minors – Who/When

- Address and resolve any hot issues

- Review CEO Dashboard, Departmental Scoreboards and Quarterly Expectation

Weekly – 90 Minutes – Owner, Leadership Team

- Review Departmental Scoreboards and CEO Dashboard

- Review Majors & Minors

- Review Employee & Client Retention and Satisfaction Survey data

- Address any hot issues

- Assess, resolve, execute, recognize

Daily – 15 Minutes – Everyone in the company

This is a 15-minute "daily huddle" conference call that each person in the company is on every single day, with their team and their team's leader, supervisor or manager.

- Wins, based on KPIs

- What's not working

- What's up for tomorrow

- What will be resolved – Who/When

Quarterly All Company Meetings

This is about building company culture and morale

- Where you've been

- Where you're going

- Get feedback from employees

- Discuss training

- Review issues

- Make commitments to resolve issues

- Open Q & A

Key Points for Chapter 12

- You must become financially literate. This means that you need to learn how to read, analyze and understand your key financial reports. The information on these reports will give you invaluable insight and help you make better business decisions, which in turn will help you to produce the desired outcomes.

- Use scorecards, scoreboards and dashboards to get a full view of your leading indicators (KPIs) and lagging indicators (financials), and regularly scheduled meetings to review these and keep everything on track.

Chapter 12 Exercise

Assess where you are currently at regarding having and reviewing financial and operational metrics. Is your accounting department providing financial reports on a regular basis (or do you know how to pull them yourself)? Do you have KPIs for each of your team members (or any of them at all)? How often are you having the types of meetings described in this chapter, and is this a planned schedule or a haphazard schedule?

It's always good to establish a baseline so that you can measure your progress as you implement what you are learning.

CHAPTER 13:

UNDERSTANDING THE FINANCE PILLAR,
PART 3 – TEAM BUILDING, SALES & MARKETING

Sir Richard Branson, the billionaire founder of the Virgin Group, said, "A company's employees are its greatest asset and your people are your product." This is especially true in a service business.

In Chapter 11 I said that successful businesses attract, deliver and retain both internal customers (i.e., these all-important employees) and external customers (the people and organizations that buy the products and services that your employees deliver). This chapter will dive into best practices for doing all this attracting, delivering and retaining.

Create an empowering, core-values-based community

The members of your workforce form a community. What kind of a dynamic do you want this community to have? As a leader, manager and/or owner, it is your job to create and nurture a positive, empowering community dynamic that supports your business, your employees and your customers. The axis that this community spins upon will always be its *core values*.

In Chapter 2 you learned how to identify a group's core values. If you have not yet followed this process to identify your company's core values, you need to do so now. But be aware that merely identifying your core values is not enough. What I've seen is that this is where a lot of people get the core values thing wrong. They read a book like this and think, "Wow! I found the 'magic pill'! No wonder we haven't been successful – we don't have core values!"

So they create a set of values that looks pretty on paper and call everyone together for a Big Deal Meeting where they roll out the core values to the team. Management is all excited. They even bring in a nice lunch for everyone for the occasion. Yay! Barbecue!

Then the meeting ends and everyone on the team thinks, "Okay, great, whatever," and gets back to business as usual. Two weeks later management is scratching their heads wondering why everyone is still unreliable. After all, they just announced that "reliability" is one of their core values. LOL!

The mistake here is thinking that all you need to do is identify and announce your core values. In reality, your "core values roll-out meeting" is just the starting point.

Once you've established your core values and educated everyone on what they mean and how they'll benefit the community, this is when the real work begins. Your company's leaders must each be accountable for seeing that the core values get put into action. This requires near-constant reinforcement. In Chapter 14 I'll provide some tips for what this near-constant reinforcement should look like.

Recruit and hire based on your company's core values

Recruitment, just like everything else you do, should be based on your company's core values. Why? Because whether you've got two employees or 200, there's nothing more magical than having a team of people who have common goals and values. In fact, it is absolutely critical to culture and morale.

I strongly recommend that you hire *first* based on character and values fit, and *then* based on technical expertise. Say you have to choose between two people for a position. Job Applicant A is an expert on the technical side but only a partial fit on the values side. Job Applicant B is a perfect match with your company's values but has less expertise on the technical skills. You should take Job Applicant B every time, without hesitation, because the values fit should be a non-negotiable.

You can teach a person technical skills. As their employer you are not going to change their character and values. This is why your company's core values should be front and center in your job postings, telephone screenings and in-person job interviews.

That said, it's not enough to just identify the short list of words that represents your company's core values. You also need to have an operational description of what each of the words means at your company. Plus, as a business leader, you must also be able to tell the story of the meaning behind the values, why they are so important and the role they play in your company's day-to-day operations and success.

For example, at my company one of our core values is "Care." What this means in our company is that we foster empowering relationships through care and having positive, can-do attitudes. We build these empowering relationships both internally within our team and externally with our clients. We look to hire people who in general in life are positive individuals and go-getters who like to be part of a team and find that serving others makes them feel good.

Take a structured approach to job interviews

As an employer, you or the hiring manager should never go into a job interview and just "wing it." Instead, have a clear understanding of what you're looking for and a set of questions that you will ask each applicant.

Because you are recruiting and hiring based on your company's core values, you need to look for people for whom these values resonate. How do you do this? Start by telling them about your core values and asking how these feel to them. Do they feel their own values align with these?

Because they want the job, nearly everyone will say, "Yes, of course, those are my values, too!" This is why you need to dig further. Ask a series of strategic, situational questions that force the applicant to talk about situations at one of their previous jobs where their behavior embodied each of these behaviors.

For example, based on what "Care" means at my company, here are some questions we could ask:

- Tell me about a situation at a past job in which, in the spirit of having a can-do attitude, you took care of something.

- Give me some examples of when things got tough and you needed to have a positive, can-do attitude.

- What have you done to serve or empower clients or co-workers?

- Tell me about a regular practice you have regarding taking care of yourself, taking care of clients and/or taking care of your employer's equipment. Explain to me how you've done that in the past and how you envision doing that in the future.

As the interviewee answers these questions, pay close attention to their body language and speaking pace. If they're not being completely truthful, or if they're just making the entire story up as they go, you will most likely be able to tell. They'll hem and haw and stutter. Their eyeballs will be all over the place, or they'll be consistently looking towards their right. In general (but not always), people tend to look to the left when they are remembering, to the right when they are imagining and to the right and up when they are lying.

After you have determined that an applicant is a good fit from the core values standpoint, delve into what you might think of as "normal" interview topics. What is their technical expertise for the job? How many years of experience do they have in a position that's relevant to the position you're trying to fill? Does their desired pay line up with what you're willing to pay for this position? Etc.

However, be aware that there are laws regarding things you can and cannot ask in a job interview. Some of these laws apply nationwide and some are state-specific. For example, be wary of asking about an applicant's salary history – as of this writing, 21 states prohibit employers from asking this. Some states prohibit asking about an applicant's criminal history until after a contingent job offer has been made. Some prohibit asking if an applicant is pregnant or planning to get pregnant. And the list goes on. Consult your attorney regarding the laws that apply to your business.

Regardless of what state your business is located in, *never* ask anything about the applicant's age, family, gender, marital status, nationality or religion. While you cannot ask about an applicant's medical history or disabilities, you *can* state the requirements of the job and ask the person if they can meet these requirements, with or without reasonable accommodations.

Have the final candidate come in for a paid "working interview"

Here's a little-used tactic that I strongly recommend, especially for your field technicians. Once you've identified someone that you think you want to hire, pay them to come on board for a full or half day. You'll have to work out the legalities in your state for how to make this happen.

We call these "tryouts." Take the applicant out in the field on an actual job and see how they do. This is an opportunity for you to see how they work in your work environment. What's really cool is it's also an opportunity for them to meet some of the other employees, interview you and get a feel for if your company really is a good fit for them.

If the working interview goes well, move forward with a formal offer letter and welcome them to your team.

I recommend that you take a similar approach when hiring office staff as well.

Make a good first impression with your onboarding process

First impressions are everything with humans, so get things off to a good start by having a clean, concise and highly organized onboarding process. What will they do when they first show up? Can you have all their human resources and payroll paperwork in a nice, organized folder for them? What will their training agenda be?

A lot of companies get this wrong. A new hire comes on board and the company is not prepared. Things aren't organized. They don't have any training guides or manuals. There's no training agenda laid out. And so forth. As a result, the employee feels that chaos or disorganization, and it sets a very bad first impression. Remember, they're already feeling kind of nervous coming into a new atmosphere. When you make it chaotic, this just adds to the new employee's anxiety. It makes them feel uncomfortable and uncertain – and leaves them wondering if they made the right decision to take this job.

Instead, have an organized and structured onboarding process that makes the new employee feel comfortable and at home, confident that your company will be a fabulous place to work.

If the employee will be working in the office, have their desk clean and set up with whatever equipment and supplies they need to do their job. Have their computer logins set up and ready to go. Have their email account set up. Have a "welcome aboard" card, gift or balloons waiting for them at their workstation. Go the extra mile to make them feel special, welcome and set up for success.

If the person will be working out in the field in a company truck, have this truck stocked, washed and full of gas. Have their field supervisor there to meet them and onboard them on their first day of work. Give them a vision of what their first days or weeks will look like in terms of the training program and agenda, so they'll know where they're headed.

Have weekly check-ins with new hires

Here's another thing that few companies think to do. For a new hire's first 60 to 90 days on the job, the owner/manager/leader should check in with the person once a week. How are things going? What's working? Do they need anything?

Note that this check-in should *not* be done by the person's supervisor. This is something that should be done by a manager who is above that supervisor, or by the highest person in the company.

It's just a five-minute call that pays a lot of dividends. If you're that leader, put these calls on your calendar so you do not forget to make them.

Have a formal training and development program

Regardless of how small or large your business is, you should have some type of formal training and development plan in place for every position in the company. You can find my detailed advice for making this happen in Chapter 14.

Market your business

You know the old saying, "If you build it, they will come"? Well, don't expect that to apply to your business. If you don't take action to let prospective customers know that your business exists, don't expect them to find out on their own. You need to market your business.

Marketing refers to the things you do to promote your products and services and let people who are looking for what you're selling know that you exist. Marketing is about getting your phones ringing by attracting prospective customers to your company.

While there are many possible marketing tactics that you can use, here are some that I recommend:

- **Website** – This is a must. You need a good, clean, concise, professional and educational website. It should be well written, professionally designed and super easy to navigate.

- **SEO** – Search engine optimization (SEO) is all about "optimizing" your website so that when people in your service area are online searching for what you're selling, your website comes up on page one of their search results. SEO is based on "keywords" and "keyword phrases," which are the words that people are entering into the search engine or speaking to their virtual assistant (such as Siri) during their search. SEO is more of a long play, as it can take a long time to get traction.

  A really important thing to know here is that you need to be sure you're optimizing on the right words. For an obvious example, if you're selling *commercial* HVAC services, it doesn't do you any good to come up as number one for "best *residential* air conditioning repair company near me."

- **Pay-per-click advertising** – I've found that with the right keywords, Google ads work well. Either learn how to do this yourself, or hire an expert to do it for you.

- **Yelp** – If you're selling to the residential market, running Yelp ads and getting your happy customers to post glowing reviews on Yelp can both pay off.

- **Direct mail** – If you're selling to the residential market, postcards or mailers still work. Even in business-to-business sales, with so much attention currently focused online, old-school tactics like direct mail can often cut through the noise.

- **Newsletters and blogs** – This can be a great way to showcase your expertise, stay top-of-mind with customers and prospects, and help your website's SEO (because Google likes to see that you regularly add fresh content to your site).

One way to approach this is to send out a newsletter every two to four weeks. Have each issue feature one short (approximately 400 to 500 words), well-written educational article, such as "How to Properly Program Your Thermostat to Save Energy and Money." Put the article in the body of the email rather than expecting people to click through to somewhere else.

If you make your newsletter educational, people will read it. If it's just an advertisement, they'll unsubscribe.

Then post these exact same articles on a blog on your website, and post "teasers" about these blogs on your social media pages, to entice people to click through to your website to read the blog.

- **Marketing agencies** – If you decide to hire an agency, be warned that a lot of these places are either dishonest or don't know what they're doing. Do a boatload of research on their credibility before signing up! I probably wasted $100,000 or more on bad marketing agencies that said all the right things and made lots of great promises, but did not deliver.

Finally, be aware that marketing takes time. You need a strategy and a budget, you need to be consistent, and you need to use multiple tactics at once. The results come with time and consistency.

Build a sales team

While marketing is about attracting prospective customers to your company, if you really want to scale your business you *also* need to have one or more salespeople proactively going out and finding customers and closing deals. You can only grow so fast with marketing tactics. Even if it's just a team of one, you need a sales team.

The most important thing here is to hire people with the right characteristics and attitude. You do not want people with the "order taker" mindset on your sales team. You want salespeople who are hunters and characteristically very hungry, like "animal hungry," so that they will fight for results. Your salespeople should be highly competitive, highly money motivated, not afraid to make cold calls, not afraid of rejection and not likely to give up.

Your salespeople also need to be likable. People ultimately buy from people they like and trust. This means your salespeople need to have some personality and be able to build relationships with prospective customers.

There are assessment tools you can use to determine a person's motivators and personality characteristics. These are helpful for recruiting as well as for looking at your current sales team to ensure you have the right people in the right seats at your company.

In addition to personality issues, you also need to assess technical knowledge. This is especially the case if you're serving the commercial market. Your salespeople need to be able to go out to prospective customers' facilities to identify areas of opportunity, and be able to speak intelligently with the decision maker, often on a very technical level. While you can train people on product-specific knowledge, you need to hire people who already have enough industry experience so that they're not starting from scratch.

Pay your salespeople appropriately

Aim to find the sweet spot of the right base salary to attract and retain good, hungry sales reps, paired with a commission structure that keeps them fighting for sales and closing deals. If you set the base salary high enough for them to be able to live very well, they won't be hungry enough to chase the sales in order to get the commissions that go with the sales.

Set your salespeople up for success

Getting the right person(s) on the team is the hard part. After that it's all about having a step-by-step sales process in place that your salespeople follow over and over and over again. But before you have your salespeople start selling, there are things that *you* need to do in order to set them up for success:

- **Buy a list of prospective customers.** There are list brokers that sell this information. You can get very specific and nail down the geography, industries, building type or size, company or household revenue and more.

- **Get a good CRM software system in place.** CRM stands for Customer Relationship Management. Your salespeople will need an easy way to track leads, prospects, proposals and clients. Some systems even have the ability to build out a quote, which is ideal. Your goal is to make things easy and seamless for your sales reps, so they can spend their time selling rather than pushing paperwork.

- **Create specific, measurable goals.** With salespeople it's very important that right off the bat you set goals and KPIs for their performance. Otherwise they'll waste a bunch of time not getting anything done.

  How many dials and new appointments should they have per week? How many proposals should they be presenting each month? What should their closing ratio be? How much dollar volume in sales are they expected to close each month for each type of service that you offer?

- **Ensure your operations team is strong.** Your sales reps are going to be working very hard to get sales. It is vitally important that your operations team does an excellent job of effectively and efficiently delivering the services that your reps sell, including providing a high level of timely communication with the customer.

  If your operations team is not delivering, this will scare the hell out of your salespeople. They do not want to risk losing the customers that they fought so hard to get. So instead of being out there hunting and selling, they'll go into 9-1-1 mode and get caught up in being the customer service problem solver – which is not want anyone wants.

- **Create and implement a repeatable sales process.** I lay out the details of what works at my company in Chapter 14.

Key Points for Chapter 13

- You should create an empowering, core-values-based community.

- Recruiting, hiring, training, rewarding and reprimanding should all be based on your company's core values.

- Your marketing program attracts prospective customers to your company, while your sales team proactively goes out and finds customers and closes deals. You need both.

Chapter 13 Exercise

Create and implement an anonymous survey to get your employees' perspective on your company's current culture and atmosphere. Is it uplifting and empowering? Or is it frustrating, demotivating, etc.? Is it a great place to work or does it suck?

CHAPTER 14:

IMPLEMENTING THE PRINCIPLES OF THE FINANCE PILLAR

By now your head is probably spinning. I know. I get it. I just pointed a firehose at you in Chapters 11, 12 and 13 and blasted you with all this information about systems and structure and finance and on and on and on. Sure, you'd love to get your business running like a high-performance machine. But this is so incredibly overwhelming, where the heck do you start?

Here's what you do: You identify the key areas where your business is struggling the most, and start there. And to help you out, I've created a High Performance Business Checklist that lists out all the tactics and systems that we recommend you implement, so you can check them off as you go.

Use the QR code below or go to www.BlueCollarKing.com/resources to download this checklist now.

Create your Vision Execution Map

I've created an interactive template that you can use to create your Vision Execution Map. To download this template, use the QR code below or go to www.BlueCollarKing.com/resources.

Learn how accounting works

If you do not yet understand how accounting works, or are just a little fuzzy on the concepts, there's an excellent book that I highly recommend: "The Accounting Game: Basic Accounting Fresh from the Lemonade Stand," by Darrell Mullis and Judith Orloff. This book covers all the big financial concepts associated with running a business in a way that's incredibly easy to understand.

Analyze your financial reports

In Chapter 12 you learned the basics of how your financial reports work. Now that you understand this, it's time to take a close look at yours. Analyze the numbers. What are these reports telling you about the state of your business? How do your key metrics, such as gross margin and net profit, compare to the numbers I said you should be shooting for?

Your goal should be to use your financial reports to help run your business and make both short-term and long-term business decisions. Based on your analysis of the numbers, what changes need to be made? Where should you be investing money for maximum impact? Where are you wasting money? Running your business "lean and mean" is a never-ending journey of optimizing processes, cutting unnecessary costs and making every aspect of your business more efficient.

Create your KPIs

The art of creating meaningful Key Performance Indicators generally involves some reverse engineering. What is the desired end result? What are all the steps necessary to achieve this end result?

For example, say you are trying to create KPIs for your salespeople, and your desired result is $100,000 in sales per person per month. If you have two salespeople, a KPI for the person in charge of your Sales Department might be "$200,000 in sales each month."

The KPIs for the salespeople, though, need to be more granular. What is it going to take for them to reach this target?

- **How many proposals** do they need to produce and put in front of potential clients? If you know that your average salesperson has a 33% closing rate, this means each salesperson needs to get proposals for $300,000 worth of work in front of prospects each month.

- **How many qualified appointments** are required to get those opportunities to submit proposals? To calculate this number you'll need to know (a) the percentage of appointments that usually turn into requests for proposals (a good guess is 33%) and (b) the average dollar value of your company's proposals.

- **How many cold calls** are required to get the desired number of appointments (if your company relies on cold calls)? In my company I know from history that if I have a salesperson making 15 to 20 cold calls per hour, this should result in one appointment every hour. When calculating the KPI for cold calls, though, you need to allow time in the salesperson's day to actually go out on those appointments, create and deliver proposals, and then follow up and close sales.

In this example there are four KPIs you can create to measure the daily and weekly activity of your sales reps to see how many calls they're making, how many appointments they're setting, how many appointments are converting into opportunities to present proposals, and then how many of these proposals are turning into sales.

When you do this, you'll be able to look at these KPIs – these leading indicators – and tell within the first few days of the month where your sales will be in 30 to 60 days.

Creating meaningful KPIs for every function in your company is not always as straightforward as creating them for your sales team, but the basic concepts are the same.

Create your Accountability Chart

Once you have KPIs for each function, the next step is to create your Accountability Chart. Remember, the Accountability Chart shows who reports to who, like on an Organizational Chart, but it also shows what each person is responsible for and the KPIs on which their performance will be measured.

You can download an editable template for creating your Accountability Chart at www.BlueCollarKing.com/resources or by using the QR code below.

Create your scorecards, scoreboards and CEO dashboard

You'll find some helpful tools and templates for doing this at www. BlueCollarKing.com/resources or by using the QR code below.

Set your meeting cadence/rhythm

I provided an outline of what works at my company in Chapter 12. Decide how often you will hold your meetings and then establish regular days and times for these meetings and get them on the calendars of everyone involved.

Constantly reinforce your core values

Here's what I've seen works well:

- **Have everyone memorize your core values.** Everyone in your organization should be able to easily recite them. You can even distribute pocket cards the size of business cards that are printed with these core values, to make it easy to always have them handy.

- **Start your daily team huddles with your core values.** In my company we have a chain of command in which each team member reports to a supervisor, with no more than six or eight employees per leader. At 3:30 every afternoon, every supervisor runs a 15-minute "huddle call" with their team. The first thing they do on this huddle call is have someone recite the core values.

- **Begin all formal meetings with your core values.** Your weekly, monthly, quarterly and annual meetings should all start this way. In addition, you should talk about your core values in your leadership meetings to ensure that each of your leaders clearly understands what these values mean, the difference they make and how they are implemented in your company.

- **Hire by your core values.** As discussed in Chapter 13, your core values need to be front and center in your entire recruitment process.

- **Coach, discipline and provide recognition based on your core values.** When someone does not live up to the core values you need to hold them accountable. Even more importantly, when someone *does* exhibit values-based behaviors, you need to notice!

In fact, I think it is in the area of recognition that the real magic happens. Most managers and leaders are good at catching people doing something wrong. They also need to be constantly looking for opportunities to catch people doing something *right*, i.e., behavior that aligns with your core values.

At my company we have an ongoing "all company" group chat that everyone in the company is on. At the end of each day, every leader is required to make a shout out on that group chat about at least one person on their team, highlighting how that person lived out one or more of our core values that day.

In addition to this chat-based recognition, every person in the company is encouraged to recognize values-based behaviors when they see it. This creates a lot of positive, fun energy in the culture.

Remember, as a leader your job is to coach people up in your organization. Most people respond much better to praise than they do to criticism. Focusing on core values gives you lots of opportunities to offer praise.

Why is all this so important? Because in order to get a group of people working together, trusting each other and supporting each other to achieve a common goal there must be some guiding principles. Your core values are these guiding principles. They're like an unwritten contract of how everyone will think, act, make decisions, resolve conflicts, etc. By getting everyone on the same page, your core values result in higher performance, greater camaraderie and better results.

Create a formal training and development program

As I mentioned in Chapter 13, regardless of how small or large your business is, you should have some type of formal training and development plan in place for every position in the company. I have found that regardless of the role, the training needs to be very simple, in bite-sized pieces.

Here's what I recommend:

- **Start with the job scorecard.** This should outline, in bullet point format, behavioral expectations, weekly and monthly "must do" tasks, what the functions are that this person needs to own, and the KPIs that they are accountable for.

- **Create standard operating procedures (SOPs) for each function.** Create simple instructions and SOPs for each job that tells that person precisely how they need to do each of these functions. Put these into a small training handbook.

Having these training handbooks is extremely helpful, especially if you plan to grow or scale your business. First, this gives you an agenda for training that person. Second, when the person has a question they can simply reference the handbook. This not only frees up their manager's time, it also avoids the "I didn't want to bother you" or "I was too embarrassed to ask the question" problem that inevitably leads to mistakes.

- **Create short videos demonstrating all computer-related functions.** In addition to the written training manuals, one of the things that we're now doing in my business is making training videos. These have been very successful. We're making training videos for sales, dispatch, accounting and other computer-based processes.

To do this, have team members who are already proficient at a given task use screen recording software such as Loom to make a short training video for that task. These videos combine images of the actual screens with audio of the trainer talking through each step of the process. This lets the trainee see, step-by-step, exactly what to do.

What I've seen is that a five- to 20-minute video provides a *huge* level of value. You can cover a lot of information both visually and audibly for the trainee, and they can have this to reference at any time.

Having both a written manual and short training videos dramatically condenses the time that the trainer must spend with the employee. Plus, employees love this approach because they're set up for success and have the ability to reference these materials as many times as needed.

- **Circle back to reassess after a week or two.** Here's the piece where most business owners or managers fail. Once you give your employee the tools and training materials they need, you need to check back to see how things are going. This is important because while most people will learn some things quickly and easily, they will also naturally struggle with other topics.

  Give the person a week or two to practice what they've learned. Then give them a written quiz with strategic questions around the things you wanted them to learn, and see which areas need additional training and assistance.

- **Make training and development continuous and ongoing.** Develop a culture in which the idea that "we are always getting better" is embraced by everyone in the organization. In addition to ongoing training and development, this also means encouraging everyone to get rid of the "if it ain't broke don't fix it" mentality regarding your existing SOPs and work instructions. Instead, create a culture in which everyone is always thinking about how to make things better, get more efficient, eliminate waste, provide a higher level of service, simplify things, etc.

Create a repeatable sales process

As I mentioned earlier, your salespeople need to be following a process. Here's the step-by-step sales process that has worked so well in my company. While this is specific to commercial sales, the concepts are the same for residential work.

1. **Make 150 to 200 cold calls per week** to the contacts on the list you purchased. The goal is to talk to the "gatekeeper" who answers the phone in order to identify the decision maker. Who is the executive in charge of facility maintenance?

2. **Call these decision makers.** Sometimes once the salesperson identifies the decision maker they'll immediately ask to speak with him or her. Other times they'll call the following week. Either way, the sales rep is *not* trying to sell anything over the phone.

3. **Schedule qualified appointments.** The only goal of the call to the decision maker is to get a "qualified appointment" to stop by to meet them and survey the facility to see if there is an opportunity for your company to help them.

   A "qualified appointment" is a real appointment at a specific day and time, with a key decision maker who has the authority to buy your services and who has put this appointment on their calendar. It is not a "stop by some time to drop off a brochure" or "come by when you can" agreement. It's an actual appointment.

4. **Meet with decision makers.** This is where the sales rep goes out on these appointments. Note that some training may be necessary to ensure each salesperson makes the most of each appointment. They need to be able to ask strategic questions to identify the decision maker's pain points, find out what currently is and is not working well for them, and more. While at this appointment they

also need to survey the facility, take pictures of the equipment (a picture is worth a thousand words!) and identify areas of opportunity where it appears things are not being properly maintained or can be improved.

During this meeting, the salesperson should obtain permission from the decision maker to send them a report with their findings and a proposal for any improvements or changes that they recommend.

5. **Create reports and proposals.** Next the salesperson creates a report of their findings and recommendations, complete with pictures, and a proposal for implementing these recommendations, and sends it to the decision maker. The faster this is done, the more impressed the prospective client will be with the level of service your company provides.

6. **Close sales.** This is where the rep's follow up and sales skills come in. Now they need to turn their proposals into sales.

Wash, rinse and repeat, over and over again. These are the steps that your salespeople should be following day after day, week after week, month after month.

Do fun things with your team

While the main focus of work needs to be work, it really cannot just be 100% grind, grind, grind. You need to include some fun, too.

Be sure to put fun team-building activities on the calendar. Have a time and place for each team to have lunch or go do something fun, such as driving go-karts, going to the shooting range, having a party on a yacht, or whatever would appeal to most of the team members.

This will help build cohesiveness within the community and make your company a more enjoyable place to work.

CHAPTER 15:

CONCLUSION

When you first started reading this book you may have made a beeline for the Finance section. After all, growing your business and making more money were probably the top things on your mind.

Eventually, though, you reached the same epiphany that I did: If you want to grow your business, you must also grow yourself. As I pointed out in the Preface, if you try one thing after another and nothing works, the common denominator is *you*. In order for things to change, you need to change. As Jim Rohn said, "In order for things to get better, you need to get better."

But as the Blueprint for Success has shown you, you can't just focus on growing your business and the "business side" of your life. Everything is connected and everything needs a system. If you don't also build a strong foundation and address the Faith, Family and Fitness aspects of your life, sooner or later things will fall apart anyway. Or you will just keep hitting a "business ceiling," no matter how many different systems or tactics you try. Getting to where you want to go is a holistic, all-encompassing game.

Growth and change are not easy

When they choose to step into growth, most people don't stay in long enough to get the reward. They give up and quit right before they have a breakthrough, so they never experience the expansion. They never reach that next level of the game.

Why? Because it's hard to embrace vulnerability and humility. It's hard to do the work of shifting our perspectives, responses and ways of doing things. It's hard to change. And getting pulled out of your comfort zone can be extremely uncomfortable.

I sincerely hope you've gone or will go all in implementing the Blueprint for Success, and that even if you're still in that uncomfortable place, you're committed to getting through to the other side of the chasm. Trust me, it's worth it!

If you need help, I'm here for you

Some people can read and study a book like this and then implement all the systems and processes and changes on their own. I know I'm certainly not one of those people! You may not be, either. If that's the case, having the right coach can make a world of a difference.

The right coach is someone who has experience doing what you're trying to do. Because they've already done the work, they have massive confidence – to the point where it almost scares you. They're not afraid to call you out on your bullshit and blind spots. And they're not the sort to just talk and teach at you. They'll get in the trenches with you and get their hands dirty.

In other words, someone like me. If you've read the book and had your eyes opened but feel you can use some extra guidance and assistance putting the entire Blueprint for Success into place in your business and life, I've got your back.

From Instagram reels on leadership and business management to a free Facebook group and both one-on-one and group coaching program, I offer a wide variety of tools and resources to help you get yourself and your company from where you are now to where you want to be.

To learn more about all of this visit www.BlueCollarKing.com or scan the QR code below.

Final thought

The road to transformation can be tough. But if you stay with it long enough, I promise that there will be a reward and you'll start experiencing the greater wealth, abundance, fulfillment, impact, freedom and fun that you've been so hungry for.

Now go out and be a maverick, a blue collar king. The world desperately needs more hungry, noble and courageous leaders!

ACKNOWLEDGEMENTS

I would like to thank some of the many people who have played such important roles in my journey…

To my amazing wife, Heather Murray: Thank you for being my rock. Behind every king is a true queen who is there supporting him through the darkest, hardest, most challenging times. I love you more than I can ever express.

To my coach, Sean Whalen: Thank you for cracking me wide open, shaking my universe, waking me the fuck up and then showing me through your example what it looks like to live a life of utmost truth and integrity.

To my coach, Nikki Nemorouf: Thank you for being there for me in some of my darkest and most trying times. Thank you for helping to create the mindset that I have today, showing me the pathway to becoming a better man and putting me into the next chapter of my life.

To my pastor, Keith Craft: Thank you for bringing me, Heather and my family to God, and showing me through your example what a bold, empowered, loving and successful Christian looks like.

To my friend and "brother from another mother," Steve Weatherford: Thank you being my confidante, for helping to accelerate my spiritual journey and for being such an amazing role model for how to help, coach and guide other men.

To my book editor, Linda Coss: Thank you for helping me take everything that's in this book out of my heart and soul and brain and get it into a format from which people can learn, grow and become better people. I wouldn't have been able to do it without you!

ABOUT THE AUTHOR

Over 26 years ago Matt Murray started his career in the commercial HVAC & Refrigeration field. Today he is the Blue Collar King: a highly successful business owner, entrepreneur, author, coach and consultant. As such, Matt's expertise goes far beyond "just" his technical expertise in the HVAC/R field. Matt is also an expert in mindset, personal development, leadership and business development, operations, strategic planning, sales and more.

Matt is the Founder and CEO of Evolution Mechanical, Inc., which serves the commercial and industrial HVAC/R market, and Blue Collar King Coaching & Consulting, through which he guides owners and would-be owners of service-based businesses in the blue collar trades to success both personally and professionally.

Matt is passionate about helping others live happy, successful and fulfilling lives.

An avid outdoorsman, Matt often seeks out speed- and adrenaline-filled adventures. He loves fishing, piloting high-performance boats, going off-roading, flying small aircraft (he's been a pilot since 2010), scuba diving and visiting white sand beaches. He particularly enjoys spending time with his amazing wife and children, including taking family camping trips and going off the beaten path to explore the small fishing villages of Baja Mexico.